MORNING MOTIVATION

The Ultimate Workbook & Guided Journal

Practical Wisdom to Break Free From Self-Doubt
& Start Living an Extraordinary Life

Shawn Langwell

Copyright © 2025 Northstar Communications

All rights reserved. No part of this book may be reproduced or used in any manner without the prior written permission of the copyright owner, except for the use of brief quotations in a book review. To request permissions, contact the author at shawnlangwellwriter@gmail.com

ISBN: 978-0-9982487-9-0

Editing, cover, and design by Crissi Langwell
Author photo by Stuart Lirette

ShawnLangwell.com

If you sometimes struggle with imposter syndrome, procrastination, or overthinking, and making decisions, then this book is for you. Morning Motivation is for people like us who are sick and tired of allowing fear to hold us back. It is dedicated to every brave soul willing to step through their fears and desperate or driven enough take a chance on themselves. If you're ready to be inspired, encouraged, and transformed, I'm here to guide you every step of the way.

Table of Contents

Introduction 1
Change and Getting Started 4
Writers Block 7
Addicted to Worry 10
Procrastination 13
Never Enough 16
Someday I'll… 19
If Only… 23
The Barren Desert of Doubt and Indecision 26
I Wish I Would Have…Learning to Live With No More Regrets 30
Say Goodbye to Guilt and Shame 33
No Longer Controlled by Fear, Doubt, or Insecurity 36
I am Not an Imposter 39
Brick by Brick 42
Greatness Requires Rehearsal, Trust, and Willingness to Let Go 45
To Love and Be Loved 48
We All Want to Feel Like We Belong 51
Make Your Bed and Take Out the Trash 55
Chop Wood. Carry Water. 59
Routines and Habits 62
Practice. Practice. Practice. 65
Dare to Be Great 68
Be Yourself, Always 71
Embrace Fear, Change, and the Unknown, and Do it Anyway 74
Out with the Old to Make Room for the New 78
Change is Not as Scary as You May Think 82
What's Your White-Hot Why? 85
Admit, Accept, and Adapt 89
Finding the Courage to Dream and Believe, Again 92
Dusty Dreams 95
Creating Compound Confidence is a Process 98
Gratitude, Like Happiness, is a State of Mind 102
Beware of The Comparison Trap 105
Finding Our Why 108
Big Rocks First 111
A River of Ambitions 115
Upstream 118
Go with the Flow 122

Be Here Now. 125
Courage to Change 128
Success is Whatever You Decide it to Be 131
The Power of Belief 135
Practice Daily Acts of Kindness 139
The Secret Power of Prayer, Meditation, and Visualization 142
Action, Not Words 146
Do Your Best, Always 150
I Will…Until 153
Acceptance and Detachment 156
Focus on What You Can Control and Let Go of What You Can't 160
Performance Issues: Is Giving Our Best Good Enough? 163
Massive Action 167
Confidence is a Product, Not a Prerequisite of Success 170
Crossing Bridges over Rivers of Fear and Unmet Dreams 173
The Path is the Path 176
Letting Go of Expectations 179
Love and Acceptance 183
The Disease of Loneliness: Longing to Belong 186
Creating Connection and Community 189
Find a Cause Worth Fighting For 192
Pass it On 195
Gratitude 198
Victim or Victor: Taking Responsibility For How We Feel 201
Beware of the Itty-Bitty Shitty Committee in Your Head 204
Enough! Becoming Brave Enough to Tell Your Inner Critics Off 207
Forgiveness is a Master Key to Finding Inner Peace 210
Heal Thyself: Love and Be Loved 214
Plan Your Work and Work Your Plan 217
Your Attitude Changes Everything 220
What's Your One Thing for Today? 223
Don't Overthink It 226
Your Aptitude and Worth are Not Fixed 229
Finish What You Started 233
Final Thoughts: 237
Reminders to Memorize and Do Until They Become Habits 240
Gratitude 241
About the Author 242
Other Books By Shawn Langwell 243

Introduction

This workbook and guided journal is your morning muse for an even better life than the one you've been living.

My primary goal is to help you start your day off with a better, more positive attitude than most of us typically do. To stop the morning and daily chatter of a hundred hungry chipmunks scurrying about your mind, looking for lost nuts!

You know what I'm talking about.

We all have them—*chipmunks, squirrels, and soul-sucking mind rodents*.

They are more commonly known as *fear, doubt, worry, overthinking, imposter syndrome, etc.* Many are early risers, frequently starting their incessant chatter as soon as we open our eyes, sometimes earlier. Usually, they start in well before we've had our first cup of coffee, checked our phones, or taken a morning piss.

What if you could silence those noisy little shits and reclaim some sanity and sense of control about your day and your life? How much smoother would your day be?

Well, here's your chance.

What follows are brief but impactful insights, strategies, and tidbits of inspirational wisdom that have served me well for decades and which I believe you will find helpful too.

Some of the principles, habits, or values included in this short book have taken years of practice for me to develop and master, and they seemed to flow effortlessly as I wrote them.

Others, I still struggle with. Honestly, a few are "ideals" I doubt I will ever master. And I'm cool with that. The point is to offer you tools and mindset principles that have worked for me so they may in turn encourage you to practice them and to discover your own path toward inner peace. Toward an extraordinary life not ruled by fear.

This workbook is your opportunity to flip the script in your head.

The insights in *Morning Motivation* are specifically for those who have a *growth mindset* and place a *high value on perpetual self-improvement*, especially those who a want to live happier, more productive, meaningful, and fulfilling lives. It is also for those who appreciate a good challenge, knowing and understanding that *any progress is going to be awkward at first*. It always is.

That's true for just about anything in life. From learning to swim or ride a bike to using a computer to whatever… if you want to get better at anything you must keep at it until you feel confident enough to *find your flow*.

In other words, **confidence is a product of doing, not thinking.** Later, you can decide if you want to raise the bar or learn something else. That's what makes life so freaking exciting for those with a growth mindset—we never stop learning, changing, and improving unless we give up or die.

This is your book. Your private time. There is no one here to watch or judge you. Journal, brainstorm, reflect or write about what bugs you, and what you want to change, improve, or let go of.

This is your opportunity let go of that overstuffed sack of shit you've been schlepping around, perhaps for decades. And instead, become more curious, inspired, bolder, confident, and courageous. This is your chance to blow the dust off your dreams and once again begin to believe you can step into who you were created to be, without apology.

It's time to embrace who you already are and *unleash the warrior within*.

As you consider, meditate, and respond to the inspirational prompts that follow each chapter, I encourage you to let the words sink in.

Feel them and ask yourself what they are trying to teach you *now*, in this moment.

The point of this book is to help you feel more in control of your life and the direction it's headed than ever before—purposeful, intentional, driven, clear, and alive. I encourage you to remain open, curious, honest, and vulnerable as you progress.

The prompts and worksheets I've included are specifically designed to help you shift your thinking and approach to the inevitable problems and challenges of life from a fearful mindset to one of boldness. From a scarcity mindset to abundance, whatever that means to you.

They serve as guides to help you improve your life, career, or craft so you can reclaim joy.

Journaling is one great way to examine where we are now and to manifest new realities; to change the stories about who we think we are—our identity. A chance to become more emotionally mature and find the balance so many of us crave in our stressful lives.

Meditation is equally important.

To get the most out of this workbook it is also imperative to **resist your natural urge to resolve everything immediately.**

Instead **give yourself permission to be still.**

Let your questions sit there, unanswered and unresolved.

In time, the answers you seek will be revealed. Eventually, you *will learn to trust your gut more and* ***know*** *what to do when the answers appear.*

It is in these structured and unstructured moments of being fully aware and present that our greatest discoveries about ourselves and the epiphanies and serendipities are revealed. I encourage you to honor the sacredness of this time. Use these reflective moments to *ask, listen, and follow whatever the universe is trying to tell you.*

Morning Motivation can help you *become more keenly aware of the latent wisdom and genius already simmering within you.* To get the most out of the prompts, I encourage you to gently coax your inner strength into the light giving it space to breathe through meditation or other practices.

In short, these bits of encouragement or inspiration are specifically written for you to carefully consider and incorporate into your daily life—into your beingness. All your comings and goings. Thoughts, conversations, and actions.

They are designed to help you *level up and harness the power you already have within* for the greatest good—for you as well as anyone you serve and interact with on a regular basis.

Whether applied to artistic endeavors or used to build stronger more meaningful personal and professional relationships, or simply as self-assessment and accountability tool for personal growth, this is your time to explore the next chapters of your life.

Honor yourself and meditate on what you read, allowing the words and any emotional response they evoke to settle into your bones.

Remain mindful of the multitude of opportunities that come up for you to practice what you learn from each day's reading. And **become bold enough to act on them.**

Honor this time, the process, and let it be as it is.

Remember, you are where you are as a result of the choices and decisions you've made. What you choose to do or not do is entirely in your control. I implore you to choose wisely.

This workbook is also your opportunity to write or rewrite narratives that no longer serve you and create new ones that will.

In other words, to *change your story and your life*.

Whether in this volume or any other work I choose to write or teach, I pledge to give you my very best in the moment, always.

And know this: **As long as we are committed to and actively improving a little bit every day, we cannot fail, ever.**

To me, that means completely surrendering and challenging my deep-rooted tendency to overthink everything. Perhaps you too can relate.

In your continued quest to discover a greater sense of meaning, purpose, and understanding for your life, I hope *Morning Motivation* becomes one of your best friends; an integral tool you return to often to awaken and embolden your soul and spirit; to *find, embrace, and act upon your own truth within—here, now, always.*

Though my wish is for you to completely transform your life into ways beyond your wildest dreams and aspirations, I am not attached to how you use this book or what impact it may have on the trajectory of your life. Nor do I have that power. But you do.

My main goal and mission in my life is to help you become bold enough to take a chance on you!

When you do, you cannot lose.

Whatever you gain from reading and practicing these principles is a win.

It is as it is, and that is good enough for me.

I hope it is for you as well.

Enjoy!
Love, Shawn

Change and Getting Started

There are two difficult things in life: Change and starting something new or unknown.

I wish it wasn't so. Yet no matter how many times I start to write a new book, story, or start anything new that is unfamiliar, the gremlins in my head scurry in fury, like ants, eggs in mouth, scrambling to safety, away from the flood caused by a rainstorm or sidewalk being power washed.

And then there is my incessant, nagging resistance to change. It can be anything new or different. A new environment, a new home, a new job, a new relationship, a new goal. Or deciding what to wear, eat, or what movie to see.

The fact is most of us, like the flooded ants, don't like change, especially when we don't have a choice. We like routines. Or if given the option for something new, perhaps even better, we typically choose not to change, to stay where we are because it's familiar, comfortable. That is generally not a winning formula for an abundant and fulfilling life. Nor should it be.

So rather than risking our pride because we will likely suck at something new, we play it safe, living in the same childhood neighborhood, wearing the same clothes and having our favorite dish at a local eatery. But does familiarity make us happy? Or does it get boring?

What prevents us from taking the bold first step toward something we think we want, or from trying something new? I don't know. I suspect there are hundreds of reasons for each of us. I do know this, the greatest opportunities for a richer, more fulfilling life, if that's what we want, are not to be found drowning in the flooded tunnels of comfort and familiarity.

To feel fully alive and thrive, we must continue to learn, grow, and evolve, or we risk drowning in a puddle of mediocrity.

Today is all we have. And today is a great day to take a chance on you and make the decision to step into your fear of the vast unknown and trust that you will not drown. Today, is the first day of the rest of your life. I hope you make the most of it.

Room to Write, Reflect & Respond

Consider these questions/prompts when and where they're appropriate:

What does this prompt stir in you?

Positive	Negative

What resistance, if any do you feel and where?

For example: Before I speak or make cold-calls I feel a knot in my throat and tightness in my belly.

Old Story	New Story

What if... Consider the worst-case scenario and ask yourself if it's likely to happen or just fear. Then reframe each problem/challenge into an opportunity.

Evaluate the Risks & Rewards of Action/Inaction

Risk	Reward

Action	Inaction

If what you want is necessary and important, decide to act right now.
If not, let it go. Unless or until it becomes important, it's not and is an energy drain.

Ask and Commit

What **one thing** can you do to change/let go of/advance that will make you happier and bring you peace and joy?

Thoughts:

Feelings:

Potential Actions:

Finally, write a Positive Affirmation/Mantra that will help support and manifest your ideal new story.

For example: My success is inevitable. It feels great to have a regular exercise routine. I sleep well and am grateful every day.

Writers Block

Writing a book is nerve wracking. When I got up this morning, I had all these grand ideas that I outlined in my journal. "I got it!" I exclaimed out loud at 7:15 a.m. Hours later, I sat staring at a blank page, all my inspiration vanished. Then I had an idea and my wife interrupted, "I'm going now. See you soon."

"Goodbye. See you later, I'm trying to write now," I snapped, turning away as she snuggled up for a kiss.

"You haven't written anything yet," she said, glancing at my blank screen. She's a writer too and it was all in jest, but for a moment I was irritated, not from her playful affection, but because getting started is so freaking hard. Then when I finally had a thought, she joked again, walking down the stairs, "Goodbye! I'll miss you," then giggled as I heard the door click.

She gets it and knows all about writer's block. But some people are just better at tuning things out and staying focused when it comes to creative endeavors.

Not me.

I need quiet. Solitude. Freedom to think without interruption. And I still struggle with second guessing things after I do finally get started. Does any of this sound familiar?

Therein lies another problem—*perfectionism*. In the beginning of writing a new book, I have so many thoughts and ideas bouncing around my brain like a BB in a steel drum. I just want one. One I can explore, unpack and add some color to that sounds inspiring, encouraging, helpful. It has to be just right. And *it will be when I let go of trying to make it perfect. When I stop thinking about what I want to say and just start writing.* I know this. I've done it many times. In fact, the best way to get over writer's block is—wait for it—to write!

How deeply profound! And yet so true. As with doing anything we are afraid of at first. Why do you think the Nike slogan is so powerful? Because, **doing is where the magic happens**.

For those of you who struggle with getting started, who want to write a book but haven't even started, who want to do (fill in the blank), I offer this deep pearl of wisdom: *Just freaking do it!*

If you want to write, write. If you want to lead, lead. If you want to change jobs, start looking for one you may like, send a resume, and wait. Whatever it is that stands in your way, the best thing you can do is not to wait until the planets are aligned on a super moon Monday. Instead, get busy living instead of worrying about all the things that might go wrong.

Today is the perfect day to take a chance on you. Just say yes and get to it. You'll be glad you did.

Room to Write, Reflect & Respond

Consider these questions/prompts when and where they're appropriate:

What does this prompt stir in you?

Positive	Negative

What resistance, if any do you feel and where?

For example: Before I speak or make cold-calls I feel a knot in my throat and tightness in my belly.

Old Story	New Story

What if... Consider the worst-case scenario and ask yourself if it's likely to happen or just fear. Then reframe each problem/challenge into an opportunity.

Evaluate the Risks & Rewards of Action/Inaction

Risk	Reward

Action	Inaction

If what you want is necessary and important, decide to act right now.
If not, let it go. Unless or until it becomes important, it's not and is an energy drain.

Ask and Commit
What **one thing** can you do to change/let go of/advance that will make you happier and bring you peace and joy?

Thoughts:

Feelings:

Potential Actions:

Finally, write a Positive Affirmation/Mantra that will help support and manifest your ideal new story.

Addicted to Worry

"Will this matter five years from now?" My stepfather David asked me this deep and disarming question over thirty years ago when I came to him with some worries and doubts, I had about my job and career path.

According to several studies, 85-92% of the things we waste precious time worrying about will never happen. Why then do so many of us still worry?

Great question. I don't know. There are no clear-cut answers. But like many bad habits or addictive tendencies, it serves a purpose, until it doesn't.

What do I mean? Our tendency to worry is a means of coping with potential negative consequences. When we are prepared to be disappointed (worry), the pain of not getting what we want is lessened. Worry may be helpful in the short term, but when it's our primary default response to any fear or anxiety, it can be costly.

Escape and avoidance are seldom a healthy response to fear. Numbing our anxiety or discomfort with some form of escape such as binge-watching Netflix cuddled up with a pint of Ben and Jerry's Chunky Monkey 'til two in the morning on a work night is not going to make your fears go away. Neither will shopping, sex, drugs, or alcohol, or incessant worry. In fact, not facing the root causes of what we tend to worry about will only exacerbate, not eliminate, our problems.

Who wants that? Not me.

So, what's the solution? There are many. One of the simplest is *to pay attention to how you feel and what you do when you feel anxious, uncomfortable, and start to worry*. Sit with your feelings for a moment and don't try to avoid, numb, replace, or ignore them. Then ask yourself three simple questions:

1) How real is this thing I am worrying about?
2) What's the worst thing that can happen and how likely is that to occur?
3) Will this "big thing" I'm all worried about really matter five years from now?

If so, seek professional help. If not, then **let it go.**

Room to Write, Reflect & Respond

Consider these questions/prompts when and where they're appropriate:

What does this prompt stir in you?

Positive	Negative

What resistance, if any do you feel and where?

For example: Before I speak or make cold-calls I feel a knot in my throat and tightness in my belly.

Old Story	New Story

What if... Consider the worst-case scenario and ask yourself if it's likely to happen or just fear. Then reframe each problem/challenge into an opportunity.

Evaluate the Risks & Rewards of Action/Inaction

Risk	Reward

Action	Inaction

If what you want is necessary and important, decide to act right now.

If not, let it go. Unless or until it becomes important, it's not and is an energy drain.

Ask and Commit

What **one thing** can you do to change/let go of/advance that will make you happier and bring you peace and joy?

Thoughts:

Feelings:

Potential Actions:

Finally, write a Positive Affirmation/Mantra that will help support and manifest your ideal new story.

Procrastination

Procrastination is another form of worry. It's rooted in fear. It's often a symptom of a much larger problem but it's not always bad.

What do I mean? Sometimes we need to put things off because they are not as important as others. I think our real problem isn't our tendency to procrastinate. Rather, it's not feeling in control of our time, money, or things we say we want to do. We lack clarity, motive, direction, and discipline. When we are not clear about what we want, we waffle. We procrastinate. It's perfectly normal. But normal doesn't mean it's healthy. A healthier response would be to intentionally come up with a plan, ask for help, or delegate and drive the results you want to accomplish. Seems simple and obvious, right?

Unfortunately, too many of us pretend to be ostriches, hiding our heads in the sand rather than having the guts to make meaningful decisions, to take control of our own future. Instead, we hide. We procrastinate. As a result, we feel frustrated and unproductive, further perpetuating a negative downward spiral of laziness and apathy, and for some, impending doom.

Recently, a "How to Overcome Procrastination" Mastermind Course ad hit my Facebook feed. It asked a simple, but normal question: *Want to learn the five secrets to overcoming procrastination? Click here…*

While there are many more levels to overcoming procrastination, I couldn't help myself, I had to comment: "Want to know the quick and easy way to stop procrastinating?

Do something!"

Needless to say, the author/entrepreneur fought back, arguing about the need to think before you act, and a whole bunch of other things, none particularly untrue.

But they missed the point: Once you have found some clarity about what you want and what benefit will come from whatever it is you say you want to do, the ONLY way to move past your procrastination habit is by taking action.

In short, stop thinking and do something positive and productive, now.

Room to Write, Reflect & Respond

Consider these questions/prompts when and where they're appropriate:

What does this prompt stir in you?

Positive	Negative

What resistance, if any do you feel and where?

For example: Before I speak or make cold-calls I feel a knot in my throat and tightness in my belly.

Old Story	New Story

What if... Consider the worst-case scenario and ask yourself if it's likely to happen or just fear. Then reframe each problem/challenge into an opportunity.

Evaluate the Risks & Rewards of Action/Inaction

Risk	Reward

Action	Inaction

If what you want is necessary and important, decide to act right now.
If not, let it go. Unless or until it becomes important, it's not and is an energy drain.

Ask and Commit

What **one thing** can you do to change/let go of/advance that will make you happier and bring you peace and joy?

Thoughts:

Feelings:

Potential Actions:

Finally, write a Positive Affirmation/Mantra that will help support and manifest your ideal new story.

Never Enough

It's sad to see people with great skill and passion self-destruct when faced with something new or uncomfortable. Or worse, to stay where they are playing their favorite head game, "Never enough." Or similar games, "If only," "Someday I'll," and "I wish I woulda."

Newsflash: in the beginning of anything new, we all suck. And the sooner we accept that fact, the sooner we can start focusing on finding the courage or willingness to face our inner critics.

I know this may sound harsh, but how many times a day do we succumb to the "itty bitty shitty committee" between our ears? You know, the voices the inner critics with their incessant chatter who survive and thrive on the nonsense we feed them.

Every self-deprecating thought, excuse, or false rationale that we tell ourselves about why we aren't good enough, smart enough, thin enough, rich enough, young enough, etc. ad nauseous infinitum… At some point, if we are to break free from this insidious cycle and bad habit, doesn't it make sense that we'll need to do something different? But what?

I don't know what *it* is for you. For me, it's getting sick and tired of letting fears control who I am and what I want to be or do. It may seem totally obvious to some, but the quickest, fastest, and most effective way I know to break free from the handcuffs of my own fears, doubts, and insecurities is to first *recognize them* when they pop up. To *sit with my uncomfortable feelings* for a bit.

Then I ask myself, **how badly do I want to <u>not be controlled by my inner critics</u>? More importantly, what am I gonna do about it?**

Ouch… I know. But it's true.

Somewhere in this process I usually find a reason and motivation to feel the fear and take a chance on me anyway. When I do, something magical happens, almost instantly. Whether I succeed or fail—I quickly discover that *I can*. All I have to do is be willing to do something different and not get hung up on the results (getting what I wanted) immediately.

When I find the courage to take action *and* let go of my attachment to the outcome, I win. Every time. And my confidence skyrockets because I am no longer a prisoner of my own limitations.

Practice this process of awareness and new action. I can almost guarantee you will feel better when you do.

Room to Write, Reflect & Respond
Consider these questions/prompts when and where they're appropriate:

What does this prompt stir in you?

Positive	Negative

What resistance, if any do you feel and where?
For example: Before I speak or make cold-calls I feel a knot in my throat and tightness in my belly.

Old Story	New Story

What if... Consider the worst-case scenario and ask yourself if it's likely to happen or just fear. Then reframe each problem/challenge into an opportunity.

Evaluate the Risks & Rewards of Action/Inaction

Risk	Reward

Action	Inaction

If what you want is necessary and important, decide to act right now.
If not, let it go. Unless or until it becomes important, it's not and is an energy drain.

Ask and Commit

What **one thing** can you do to change/let go of/advance that will make you happier and bring you peace and joy?

Thoughts:

Feelings:

Potential Actions:

Finally, write a Positive Affirmation/Mantra that will help support and manifest your ideal new story.

Someday I'll...

When I published my second book, *Ten Seconds of Boldness,* I had several friends reach out to me and ask how I did it. They had books they wanted to write, too, but didn't know where to start.

At first, I wondered why they would be reaching out to me. After all, I'd only written two books. My wife has written more than a dozen. Then it occurred to me—I did something they hadn't yet. I had moved from "Someday, I'll" to "I'm glad I did," and now others wanted some tips and encouragement to turn their stories into books.

I'll admit, it was flattering that they asked, but inside I kind of felt ill equipped to help them. I was by no means an expert. Instead of diving into solutions, I asked them what they wanted to write about. What stories did they want to tell? How far along were they?

It turns out, each had bones of personal stories about their struggles and how they changed. But they had not yet fully outlined or walked through the narrative arcs of beginning middle or end. So, rather than give them all the publishing tips and tricks I've learned in the past six years, I offered suggestions based on what I've learned so far—the basics of story structure, and of flow and passion, and encouraged them to go finish writing their stories.

Some wanted more. They, like me, wanted a magic bullet to help them go from a book idea to actually publishing one, as soon as possible.

Life doesn't work like that.

To turn our "Someday I'll" dreams into reality requires several things: *Willingness to learn, patience, practice, time, and effort.*

Intuitively we know this. Yet, most of us are impatient and want results yesterday. One of my "Someday I'll" dreams is to become a life coach. To make it happen, I have to study, practice, and put in the time.

One of my friends wanted some coaching for writing her story. Long story short, despite not having any formal training, we agreed to meet.

After three hours of asking questions and guiding her to her own discovery, I walked away feeling better about my own ability to coach. I had never formally done it. Yet she said that she got so much out of it. She has yet to continue writing, but the point is that she walked away believing a little more in her ability that she can, and so did I.

For her, "someday" may not be today. But on that rainy day in January, she took one bold step forward and shared intimate details of her life that she had never shared before. What a privilege to hear her story! I had known her all through high school, but never really knew her until we sat down to talk about her "someday."

The point is, we all have hundreds of dreams and goals and aspirations of things we'd like to do, want to do—a-hundred-and-one "Someday I'll" dreams. Until we find the drive to earnestly pursue them, they will forever remain in a fancy box with the words, "Someday, I'll" emblazoned in gold near the latch. There they will remain until we decide, *It's time. Someday is today.*

Until then, let them rest. No guilt. No shame. They will be there whenever we are ready to find the motivation and courage to act upon them.

When that time comes, we'll know. And when it does, there are many professionals available to bring our dreams into focus and eventually a reality. All we have to do is find them.

Is your someday today?

Room to Write, Reflect & Respond

Consider these questions/prompts when and where they're appropriate:

What does this prompt stir in you?

Positive	Negative

What resistance, if any do you feel and where?

For example: Before I speak or make cold-calls I feel a knot in my throat and tightness in my belly.

Old Story	New Story

What if... Consider the worst-case scenario and ask yourself if it's likely to happen or just fear. Then reframe each problem/challenge into an opportunity.

Evaluate the Risks & Rewards of Action/Inaction

Risk	Reward

Action	Inaction

If what you want is necessary and important, decide to act right now.
If not, let it go. Unless or until it becomes important, it's not and is an energy drain.

Ask and Commit

What **one thing** can you do to change/let go of/advance that will make you happier and bring you peace and joy?

Thoughts:

Feelings:

Potential Actions:

Finally, write a Positive Affirmation/Mantra that will help support and manifest your ideal new story.

If Only…

How many times have you said or thought, *If only*…? What are the most common things you say or think about? For example, if only I had more time, more money, or a better paying job; was more confident, could stop worrying so much, etc. How do you feel when you have *if only* thoughts?

Here are some of my "if only" thoughts, some of which I have accomplished. This isn't to brag. Rather, it's to show the power of manifestation and effort.

If only I had more money. Then I had money. Then it was *if only* I had a car, girlfriend, a wife, a house, a family, etc. Then I had all those things. Now as the years progress, I find myself thinking *if only* there were more hours in the day, I could write more books. *If only* I had three million dollars in the bank, I could retire and travel and do all the things I want to do, love to do.

Based on my habits of doing the work necessary to accomplish many of my previous *if only* thoughts, there's a high probability of these coming true, too.

What are your *if only* thoughts? And more importantly, what will they mean to you if you had them? I ask this last question because as we grow and mature, our path shifts. So do our motives and interests. Quite often we lose interest in selfish things and gain interest in serving others. More money, stuff, and status no longer hold the same allure as they did in our youth.

Instead, as we realize how precious and finite this dash (time) we call life really is, most of us seek out more fulfilling and meaningful *if only* thoughts, such as experiences, closer relationships, and quality time with loved ones and friends. These in turn, fuel our passion to live a more joyous, rich, and abundant life. One where we connect more. Experience more. Love more. As we move our *if only* thoughts into soul filling experiences, our life is enhanced and enriched.

Again, I ask, what are your *if only* thoughts and when will you start turning them into fond memories?

Room to Write, Reflect & Respond

Consider these questions/prompts when and where they're appropriate:

What does this prompt stir in you?

Positive	Negative

What resistance, if any do you feel and where?

For example: Before I speak or make cold-calls I feel a knot in my throat and tightness in my belly.

Old Story	New Story

What if... Consider the worst-case scenario and ask yourself if it's likely to happen or just fear. Then reframe each problem/challenge into an opportunity.

Evaluate the Risks & Rewards of Action/Inaction

Risk	Reward

Action	Inaction

If what you want is necessary and important, decide to act right now.

If not, let it go. Unless or until it becomes important, it's not and is an energy drain.

Ask and Commit

What **one thing** can you do to change/let go of/advance that will make you happier and bring you peace and joy?

Thoughts:

Feelings:

Potential Actions:

Finally, write a Positive Affirmation/Mantra that will help support and manifest your ideal new story.

The Barren Desert of Doubt and Indecision

As previously mentioned, most of us struggle with low self-esteem and confidence in some area of our lives. We allow fear to block us from achieving our dreams and fully experiencing a life filled with meaning and purpose. We become stuck in the land of doubt and indecision. Stuck in a barren desert, under the blazing sun, where all we want is a drink of water. But, surrounded by sandy dunes, we feel lost, trapped with no guideposts to show us which way to go.

Though we are not lost in a desert at all, we still wander aimlessly, listening to the inner voices that say *we can't* rather than search for the ones that say *we can*. We believe the voices that tell us that we aren't smart enough, skilled enough, or lack the necessary courage to break free from whatever is holding us back.

Rather than risk our pride or ego to face our fears, or perhaps because our need to be perfect is greater that our want, need, or desire for change, we choose to give up before we are even halfway there. Wherever *there* is. Instead, we listen to and believe the voices in our head that scream, "You could never do that." We play it safe, the voice wins, we settle for average, and then we die. Full of regret and a whole lot of "I wish I woulda" and "if only."

To me, that is not a life. That's a prison sentence in a jail built from self-imposed fear. One where we have consciously or unconsciously shackled ourselves to a wall in a dark, cold cell of lost opportunity, or addiction, or self-doubt, effectively slamming the door on our hopes and dreams. *The worst part is that we hold the key to escape whenever we want but all too often, we choose not to use it.*

Freedom is in our grasp, but like a circus elephant, we stay tethered to a stake by a thin line because we believe we can't break free. How crazy is that? Not really, because it happens all the time. In fact, it's normal because we either haven't learned the requisite tools to flip the script in our minds or developed the habit and discipline to apply incremental changes to how we think and what we do.

The answers we desperately want are closer than most of us may realize. If we look closely at the totality of our experience, we may quickly notice that all we have been searching for has been there all along, in the six inches between our ears. In our mind, our body, and our soul. All three minds. Woven into the fabric of our being. We simply must learn to listen when each speak to us. For the answers to blossom and enrich our lives, we must learn to build confidence and trust, and, most importantly, stop believing all the lies we've told ourselves for years about our sense of worth or inadequacies.

The fact is, we can change the way we think and respond to our inner critics. It's not easy. It takes courage, diligence, and time, but the rewards of following a process to develop a healthier mindset are immeasurable.

I can say this with confidence because I've done it. I've lived through the ups and downs that are a normal part of this journey we call life and will continue to ride the proverbial rollercoaster until I die. For me, life is a series of struggles, challenges, and opportunities—valuable lessons to be learned and repeated less frequently.

Every struggle I have faced—every fear, disappointment, and unmet expectation—all have been learning experiences that presented me with a choice: *Accept what I can't change or find the courage to change what I can.*

Discovering new solutions has been and will continue to be a lifelong process. Thus far, for the past forty years, I have learned how to not panic, and stay centered in the midst of any sandstorm, self-imposed or otherwise. I understand the value of building a positive, forward-thinking mindset, and continually do things to build my own self-confidence by practicing the five key principles/habits I outlined in *Ten Seconds of Boldness*:

1. Identify the problem or opportunity
2. Clearly decide what you want
3. Know why you want it
4. Write a clear plan
5. Start working that plan

This five-step method has become a rubric for virtually any problem or opportunity I face. Since writing that book, I am more keenly aware of how I feel as I continue to battle the negative self-talk that still tries to hold me captive. I doubt my inner critics will ever completely go away. But I am far more confident knowing what to do when they attempt to hijack my process and progress.

If you ever feel the urge or need to dive deeper into any of the daily prompts or insights in this book and have not read or listened to *Ten Seconds of Boldness*, I encourage you to buy it and use it. It can have a profound impact on the trajectory of your life, as it has mine and those who've read it—several of them multiple times.

Room to Write, Reflect & Respond

Consider these questions/prompts when and where they're appropriate:

What does this prompt stir in you?

Positive	Negative

What resistance, if any do you feel and where?

For example: Before I speak or make cold-calls I feel a knot in my throat and tightness in my belly.

Old Story	New Story

What if... Consider the worst-case scenario and ask yourself if it's likely to happen or just fear. Then reframe each problem/challenge into an opportunity.

Evaluate the Risks & Rewards of Action/Inaction

Risk	Reward

Action	Inaction

If what you want is necessary and important, decide to act right now.
If not, let it go. Unless or until it becomes important, it's not and is an energy drain.

Ask and Commit

What **one thing** can you do to change/let go of/advance that will make you happier and bring you peace and joy?

Thoughts:

Feelings:

Potential Actions:

Finally, write a Positive Affirmation/Mantra that will help support and manifest your ideal new story.

I Wish I Would Have...
Learning to Live With No More Regrets

Millions, if not billions of people grapple with regret. Unfortunately, for too many, the reality of all the things we wish we would have or could have done hit us when it was too late. When we are connected to tubes and wires and perhaps a machine to push air into our lungs, gasping for just one more breath of life. When we arrive there, on the final launch pad into the great unknown, it's nearly too late.

I say nearly, because as long as we have one more breath and a functioning brain and mouth, it's never too late to say five of the most powerful magic words in any language.

Yes, it may be too late to go to all your kid's recitals or sporting events. Yes, it may be too late to take that trip to Bali you've always dreamed of. Yes, it may be too late to write a book, race on the Autobahn, or soar along the Marin and Sonoma coasts in a biplane. That may be the grim reality, and you will have to accept that or add it to the overflowing pile you've already accumulated. That mountain of "I wish I wouldas."

But, if you are not at the final launch pad before your transition, you have an opportunity to live each day as if it truly is your first. With a sense of awe and wonder for all the miraculous unknown mysteries that await. And then, to live each day as if it were your last—full of love, gratitude, joy, and inner peace, for doing the best you could with what you were given.

Most important of all, as long as you are alive, it's never too late to fully experience the healing power and serenity that follows these five powerful words—"I love you," and "I'm sorry."

Today I live my life as fully as I can or want to. Why? Because I don't want to die with any regrets.

In 2005, I had an opportunity to visit my father on his deathbed. I had not seen him in several years and was shocked to see him withering away in a spotted gown, vacuous eyes fixed on a mighty oak outside his hospital room window.

We had a moment to reconnect. A moment to reflect on all the fun things I got to do with him as a kid, like slide down the brass firepole at his work, or proudly watching as he raced off to save someone's burning home, sirens blaring, thinking, "That's my dad. He's a fireman!" And to forgive him for leaving me, my mom, and two younger brothers for another woman, just before my thirteenth birthday.

But most importantly, I was able to rub his head the same way he used to rub mine after a bath as a kid, and to feel his prickly salt and pepper stubble on my check as I whispered in his ear, "Dad, I love you."

Three days later he was gone.

Room to Write, Reflect & Respond

Consider these questions/prompts when and where they're appropriate:

What does this prompt stir in you?

Positive	Negative

What resistance, if any do you feel and where?

For example: Before I speak or make cold-calls I feel a knot in my throat and tightness in my belly.

Old Story	New Story

What if... Consider the worst-case scenario and ask yourself if it's likely to happen or just fear. Then reframe each problem/challenge into an opportunity.

Evaluate the Risks & Rewards of Action/Inaction

Risk	Reward

Action	Inaction

If what you want is necessary and important, decide to act right now.

If not, let it go. Unless or until it becomes important, it's not and is an energy drain.

Ask and Commit

What **one thing** can you do to change/let go of/advance that will make you happier and bring you peace and joy?

Thoughts:

Feelings:

Potential Actions:

Finally, write a Positive Affirmation/Mantra that will help support and manifest your ideal new story.

Say Goodbye to Guilt and Shame

Guilt is doing things you know will likely cause pain because they are either unhealthy, unsafe, or flat out foolish.

Shame is what you feel either after doing something you feel guilty about or absorbing some familial, relational, moral, ethical, or pseudo righteous ideal of what you should or should not feel about choices and decisions you have made.

Neither are healthy. So how do we say goodbye to them? That's a deep question that cannot be fully explored in this small space. The easy, oversimplified answer can be distilled down to two words:

1. Honesty
2. Boundaries

First, be honest with yourself about your motives and decisions, and potential outcomes of your actions. Feel your feelings, good, bad, or indifferent. Don't avoid them or replace them with some other form of denial or escape. If you do, it will most likely cause a negative downward spiral of more guilt, self-loathing, and shame.

Avoidance is a form of fear and denial is being dishonest with yourself. If you are going to avoid anything, avoid denial and dishonesty and any behavior that causes shame or guilt.

If you want to break free of your propensity to feel guilty or ashamed, try being honest with yourself and others. That will likely alleviate 80-90% of the guilt and shame you currently experience when actively participating in your own self sabotage.

Second, set clear and healthy boundaries. This is deeply effective and requires not only honesty, but the full breadth and depth of every tool in your emotional intelligence toolbox. For example, establishing boundaries requires knowing what is and is not OK. Knowing your triggers and being able to articulate them to others in a way that is affirming and not combative. It is valuing and honoring yourself, to not be a people pleaser, or yes man or woman, to meet a set of standards that others expect of you. It is expressing compassion and empathy for others without trying to fix them, judge them, or blame them for your own feelings.

Simply put, the secret to overcoming guilt and shame can be found by fully embracing, understanding, and practicing the principles found in the Serenity Prayer: "God grant me the serenity to accept the things I cannot change, the courage to change the things I can, and the wisdom to know the difference

Room to Write, Reflect & Respond

Consider these questions/prompts when and where they're appropriate:

What does this prompt stir in you?

Positive	Negative

What resistance, if any do you feel and where?

For example: Before I speak or make cold-calls I feel a knot in my throat and tightness in my belly.

Old Story	New Story

What if... Consider the worst-case scenario and ask yourself if it's likely to happen or just fear. Then reframe each problem/challenge into an opportunity.

Evaluate the Risks & Rewards of Action/Inaction

Risk	Reward

Action	Inaction

If what you want is necessary and important, decide to act right now.

If not, let it go. Unless or until it becomes important, it's not and is an energy drain.

Ask and Commit

What **one thing** can you do to change/let go of/advance that will make you happier and bring you peace and joy?

Thoughts:

Feelings:

Potential Actions:

Finally, write a Positive Affirmation/Mantra that will help support and manifest your ideal new story.

No Longer Controlled by Fear, Doubt, or Insecurity

First off can we agree that fear, doubt, and insecurity will never completely vanish? Much like invasive crab grass, regardless of the methods and strategies we practice or our deep desire to eliminate them, they are here to stay. Well, that's not very encouraging, you may say. Yeah, you're right. Trust me, I made the mistake of seeding my front yard with Bermuda grass when I bought this house 30+ years ago. My motives were practical: I wanted a lawn that could withstand periods of drought and that would be durable. What I failed to realize is how insidious and invasive crabgrass can be. Like fear, it chokes the life out of every tomato plant or lavender bush we plant in the front yard. Despite countless attempts to sheet mulch or cut back the roots to a "manageable" safe distance, inevitably the water seeking rhizomes crawl beneath the top-soil and strangle the roots of our other plants, literally choking them to death.

So, we are now faced with more decisions—continue to seek new ways to remove or control the crabgrass lawn or live with it. This season we are not fighting it. Next year we will purchase stainless steel containers to plant tomatoes and flowers in. The crabgrass can be managed—cut away from the edges and not allowed to climb the walls of the stainless containers to infiltrate the thriving roots of healthy plants.

And so it is with fear, doubt, and insecurity; they will always be there. We need to protect ourselves from their stranglehold on our dreams and aspirations. We must learn to accept them as they are and not knowingly allow them to invade our wellbeing choking life out of us.

How?

Read *Ten Seconds of Boldness*.

Room to Write, Reflect & Respond

Consider these questions/prompts when and where they're appropriate:

What does this prompt stir in you?

Positive	Negative

What resistance, if any do you feel and where?

For example: Before I speak or make cold-calls I feel a knot in my throat and tightness in my belly.

Old Story	New Story

What if... Consider the worst-case scenario and ask yourself if it's likely to happen or just fear. Then reframe each problem/challenge into an opportunity.

Evaluate the Risks & Rewards of Action/Inaction

Risk	Reward

Action	Inaction

If what you want is necessary and important, decide to act right now.
If not, let it go. Unless or until it becomes important, it's not and is an energy drain.

Ask and Commit

What **one thing** can you do to change/let go of/advance that will make you happier and bring you peace and joy?

Thoughts:

Feelings:

Potential Actions:

Finally, write a Positive Affirmation/Mantra that will help support and manifest your ideal new story.

I am Not an Imposter

The other day I heard a podcast by a successful doctor and leader in his profession who mentioned that he too battles imposter syndrome. When his team doesn't do as he would like them to do, he feels inadequate and questions his effectiveness as a leader.

Wait, I thought leaders and professionals were above such self-sabotaging thoughts as imposter syndrome or other forms of low self-worth and esteem.

Apparently not.

I falsely assumed that this predicament was reserved for those like me who struggle to get ahead, who want more, but sometimes don't feel deserving or worthy of any short-lived success. I failed to realize those who may be considered huge successes in the eyes of others may be fighting a secret inner battle with themselves about their own self-worth and significance to others.

By being vulnerable about his own struggles with imposter syndrome this doctor helped me, and perhaps many more, simply by talking about it.

By sharing those parts of us we would rather keep private, we open ourselves to the possibilities of no longer allowing our perceived shortcomings to control us. This subtle and simple shift of perspective can become a powerful harbinger of massive personal transformation. As with any problem, it starts with identification and admission, then clarity about what we would like to do about it.

It is a perpetual process. Some of us are fortunate enough to figure this out before we die.

Room to Write, Reflect & Respond

Consider these questions/prompts when and where they're appropriate:

What does this prompt stir in you?

Positive	Negative

What resistance, if any do you feel and where?

For example: Before I speak or make cold-calls I feel a knot in my throat and tightness in my belly.

Old Story	New Story

What if... Consider the worst-case scenario and ask yourself if it's likely to happen or just fear. Then reframe each problem/challenge into an opportunity.

Evaluate the Risks & Rewards of Action/Inaction

Risk	Reward

Action	Inaction

If what you want is necessary and important, decide to act right now.

If not, let it go. Unless or until it becomes important, it's not and is an energy drain.

Ask and Commit

What **one thing** can you do to change/let go of/advance that will make you happier and bring you peace and joy?

Thoughts:

Feelings:

Potential Actions:

Finally, write a Positive Affirmation/Mantra that will help support and manifest your ideal new story.

Brick by Brick

Here's an excerpt from *Ten Seconds of Boldness* which may help a few folks on a quest for building greater self-confidence.

Building a Brick House, One Brick at a Time
"Like a mason, confidence is built *brick by brick*. One layer at a time, held together with mortar. The choices you make in life are the bricks. The mortar is your confidence, the cement that holds it all together. Without it, your structure will crumble and fall.

Every choice, every decision, every dream, every plan, goal, or problem is yet another opportunity to place a brick, secure it with mortar, and build a structure that will last a lifetime or longer. The structure is you, your life, ambitions, who you are and what you want to be."
Ten Seconds of Boldness, p. 110-111, 2022.

Room to Write, Reflect & Respond

Consider these questions/prompts when and where they're appropriate:

What does this prompt stir in you?

Positive	Negative

What resistance, if any do you feel and where?

For example: Before I speak or make cold-calls I feel a knot in my throat and tightness in my belly.

Old Story	New Story

What if... Consider the worst-case scenario and ask yourself if it's likely to happen or just fear. Then reframe each problem/challenge into an opportunity.

Evaluate the Risks & Rewards of Action/Inaction

Risk	Reward

Action	Inaction

If what you want is necessary and important, decide to act right now.

If not, let it go. Unless or until it becomes important, it's not and is an energy drain.

Ask and Commit

What **one thing** can you do to change/let go of/advance that will make you happier and bring you peace and joy?

Thoughts:

Feelings:

Potential Actions:

Finally, write a Positive Affirmation/Mantra that will help support and manifest your ideal new story.

Greatness Requires Rehearsal, Trust, and Willingness to Let Go

Every day, we are presented with a plethora of choices. Some decisions we must make are mundane, while others may impact the trajectory of the rest of our lives.

It is our responsibility to discern which demand more of our attention, and to remain focused on our objectives and motives—*what* we want and *why* we want it.

On a personal level, it is imperative to also understand and accept that it's perfectly normal for your motivation, goals, and problems to change over time. Roll with your passion, but don't be like chaff in the wind. Stay focused long enough to resolve. Long enough to understand success and failure. Remember what it feels like to win again and again, especially after overcoming many obstacles.

This iterative process will help you develop the habits of perpetual self-evaluation and assessment as you continue to keep asking yourself, *why* and *what drives me?*

Again, with practice you will become more courageous, confident, and decisive to take the next step forward.

As you do, practice the art of letting go. Do the work and let go of your attachment to the outcome. This is a major obstacle for most of us.

Many of us suffer from the illusion of control. We like to think that if we do X then we will have result Y. While that may be true in some instances, for most everyday decisions, we are not that powerful. There are too many variables at play which are beyond our control. There are subtle yet dramatic differences between effort, influence, and control.

Our experience and intellect can help us make better decisions. And our charm and leadership can help us influence others. But neither yield the power of a magic wand to create things exactly as we think we want. We cannot control people, places, or things. The sooner we accept this fact and focus on what we can control—our thoughts, attitudes, and behavior—and let go of the results, especially as leaders, the sooner we will find success.

We will find success in the process, *not* the outcome. As we continue to take risks, practice, and improve, we will begin to trust ourselves and others more.

For those on a quest for continuous personal growth, self-improvement, or greatness, we know that our best is enough. Eventually, we will not only accept this truth but may also soon master the art of doing the work and letting go of the results. When we do, our whole world will feel easy and light.

Room to Write, Reflect & Respond

Consider these questions/prompts when and where they're appropriate:

What does this prompt stir in you?

Positive	Negative

What resistance, if any do you feel and where?

For example: Before I speak or make cold-calls I feel a knot in my throat and tightness in my belly.

Old Story	New Story

What if... Consider the worst-case scenario and ask yourself if it's likely to happen or just fear. Then reframe each problem/challenge into an opportunity.

Evaluate the Risks & Rewards of Action/Inaction

Risk	Reward

Action	Inaction

If what you want is necessary and important, decide to act right now.
If not, let it go. Unless or until it becomes important, it's not and is an energy drain.

Ask and Commit
What **one thing** can you do to change/let go of/advance that will make you happier and bring you peace and joy?

Thoughts:

Feelings:

Potential Actions:

Finally, write a Positive Affirmation/Mantra that will help support and manifest your ideal new story.

To Love and Be Loved

Every human on the face of the planet has an innate need for love and acceptance. So do many animals. We all want to *belong to* something, to feel included rather than separate from. To belong to the pack, the tribe, the in crowd, the club, a community. Nobody wants to be ostracized or excluded.

So, the question we need to ask ourselves is this: What can I do to include others, and what steps can I take to feel like I belong? In other words, what can I do to be more loving to myself and others?

We cannot wait for someone to come along out of the blue and whisper, "I love you." We must take the initiative for our own wellbeing. A great place to begin is by practicing random acts of kindness to ourselves, and then to others. Start with what you say to yourself—what you think and do—then expand your kindness outward, to how you interact and treat others, *especially those different from you.*

Learning to love and be loved is a very simple inside out strategy. We do not need to complicate it. Love doesn't care how you love, only that you do and continue to love well.

What can you do today to be more loving to yourself and others? How might that help you feel you are worthy of love?

Room to Write, Reflect & Respond

Consider these questions/prompts when and where they're appropriate:

What does this prompt stir in you?

Positive	Negative

What resistance, if any do you feel and where?

For example: Before I speak or make cold-calls I feel a knot in my throat and tightness in my belly.

Old Story	New Story

What if... Consider the worst-case scenario and ask yourself if it's likely to happen or just fear. Then reframe each problem/challenge into an opportunity.

Evaluate the Risks & Rewards of Action/Inaction

Risk	Reward

Action	Inaction

If what you want is necessary and important, decide to act right now.
If not, let it go. Unless or until it becomes important, it's not and is an energy drain.

Ask and Commit

What **one thing** can you do to change/let go of/advance that will make you happier and bring you peace and joy?

Thoughts:

Feelings:

Potential Actions:

Finally, write a Positive Affirmation/Mantra that will help support and manifest your ideal new story.

We All Want to Feel Like We Belong

In the last chapter, I mentioned the importance of learning to love ourselves and others as a catalyst to perpetuate a state of belonging and acceptance. Whether we admit it or not, all of us have a deep longing to be loved and accepted—to feel like we belong. What that looks like is a matter of personal preference.

It's understandable why. We are conditioned to focus on outcomes; to believe that our worth is defined by our level of productivity and status, the amount of money we make, our zip code, the toys we have, the cars we drive, our looks, our home, our likes and followers, and platforms, etc. The list never ends.

Today I want to further explore how to create a greater sense of belonging and acceptance, not only for yourself, but also toward others. Why is this so important?

Several employee satisfaction studies show a greater emphasis is placed on internal measures of success, especially with regard to a sense of belonging and recognition. There are many studies which explore how to improve employee satisfaction, and it's not all about money.

According to the U.S. Chamber of Commerce, there are "10 ways to keep employees happy in 2023."

1. Embrace flexibility and autonomy
2. Provide incentives
3. Map-out growth opportunities
4. Work toward DEI (Diversity, Equity, and Inclusion) goals
5. Offer remote and hybrid work options
6. Improve communication
7. Focus on employees' mental health and well-being
8. Provide training
9. Make time for socialization
10. Implement employee feedback

To create healthy inclusive communities or companies requires that *all are welcome*. For the organizations and communities of the future to thrive, we must individually and collectively feel like *we belong and are accepted as we are*.

The responsibility to create this sense of belonging and acceptance rests with each individual as well as the leaders of the various communities, organizations, and companies who place a high value on inclusion.

To create this for ourselves and/or the organizations we lead means we need to be crystal clear about what we want and what purpose we or the organization serve. That will differ among every person or group. But once those questions are answered, it will create a unity and cohesive mission where individuals and the collective community have the opportunity to collaborate and serve a purpose far greater than individual or corporate self-serving interests and desires.

The real question and challenge is this: What are you doing personally or as a leader to create a welcoming and inclusive culture? And why do you want to?

Room to Write, Reflect & Respond

Consider these questions/prompts when and where they're appropriate:

What does this prompt stir in you?

Positive	Negative

What resistance, if any do you feel and where?

For example: Before I speak or make cold-calls I feel a knot in my throat and tightness in my belly.

Old Story	New Story

What if… Consider the worst-case scenario and ask yourself if it's likely to happen or just fear. Then reframe each problem/challenge into an opportunity.

Evaluate the Risks & Rewards of Action/Inaction

Risk	Reward

Action	Inaction

If what you want is necessary and important, decide to act right now.
If not, let it go. Unless or until it becomes important, it's not and is an energy drain.

Ask and Commit
What **one thing** can you do to change/let go of/advance that will make you happier and bring you peace and joy?

Thoughts:

Feelings:

Potential Actions:

Finally, write a Positive Affirmation/Mantra that will help support and manifest your ideal new story.

Make Your Bed and Take Out the Trash

Anyone else have parents who were always on your case to clean up after yourselves or do chores? Me too. What about those of us who are parents? We probably had to give or bark these same instructions to our own kids, especially teenagers—commands that likely included make your bed, clean the bathroom, or take out the trash.

And just like when we were kids, as adults there are things we must do that aren't always fun, such as cooking, cleaning, working, or paying bills. These are basic responsibilities and part of what it takes to survive as an adult. But what about other things that we know we should do or want to pursue, but don't for a myriad of reasons—most of which are likely rooted in some type of fear or laziness? For example, taxes, looking for a better job, writing a book, or exercise? What's in our way? Why do we procrastinate? How does it feel when we don't do the things we should do, or do the things we shouldn't? Not very good, right?

Here's a simple process to break your procrastination habit and begin to feel happier and more productive.

The first step is to *increase your awareness* of what you do and how you feel when you procrastinate. Look for patterns. Pay attention to unresolved problems or unfulfilled ambitions you have and how you typically respond to them. Watch for:

- Procrastination
- Denial
- Blame
- Avoidance
- Shame
- Guilt
- Fear

The second step is life changing—do something!

Into Action/Practice/Get Busy With It:
Choose one area, one skill, attitude, or belief, that's been bugging you, or that you've been procrastinating over, and make a decision to do something about it as soon as you finish reading this chapter.

It can be anything. Make your bed. Take out the trash. Start a load of laundry. Anything. The key is not to just *think* about it, but to actually *do it*. Decide what it is, then make a plan, write it down, set a date, and get started. That's how it's done. Easy, right?

Room to Write, Reflect & Respond
Consider these questions/prompts when and where they're appropriate:

What does this prompt stir in you?

Positive	Negative

What resistance, if any do you feel and where?

For example: Before I speak or make cold-calls I feel a knot in my throat and tightness in my belly.

Old Story	New Story

What if... Consider the worst-case scenario and ask yourself if it's likely to happen or just fear. Then reframe each problem/challenge into an opportunity.

Evaluate the Risks & Rewards of Action/Inaction

Risk	Reward

Action	Inaction

If what you want is necessary and important, decide to act right now.
If not, let it go. Unless or until it becomes important, it's not and is an energy drain.

Ask and Commit
What **one thing** can you do to change/let go of/advance that will make you happier and bring you peace and joy?

Thoughts:

Feelings:

Potential Actions:

Finally, write a Positive Affirmation/Mantra that will help support and manifest your ideal new story.

Chop Wood. Carry Water.

Let's take the process we started in the last chapter and go deeper. How is chopping wood and carrying water deeper than making your bed and taking out the trash?

On the surface it isn't. But it's a Zen Buddhist philosophy which promotes not only *effort before enlightenment* (chop wood, carry water), but also the commitment to the task at hand and learning to thrive and *become enlightened while in pursuit of a goal or objective.*

It may be as meditative as washing dishes is for my wife, or preparing a fine meal is for me. It nourishes and feeds the soul as we do. That is the goal. That is the objective.

With practice, we awaken our deeper selves to a level of acceptance by doing the work because it's the right thing to do in that moment, not because we *have* to. Eventually we will do it because we *want* to or *get* to. When we do, we reach a higher state of gratitude.

This heightened state of enlightenment and gratitude happens as we do. And as we continue to chop wood and carry water, we may discover even deeper levels of inner calm and serenity because we are not thinking about the buckets we must carry or the woodpiles we must build nor the reasons why we must do each. We don't need to think about why we are doing a thing, because we *know*. We need water to drink and wood to cook or stay warm. We do it because it is the right thing to do.

And so it is with any task that may seem uncomfortable or inconvenient; we must do them until we learn to see the bigger picture and fully trust that by doing, we become awakened to a deeper meaning, and we will trust that we are right where we need to be as we continue to chop wood and carry water. As we do, we remain grateful that we can.

Room to Write, Reflect & Respond

Consider these questions/prompts when and where they're appropriate:

What does this prompt stir in you?

Positive	Negative

What resistance, if any do you feel and where?

For example: Before I speak or make cold-calls I feel a knot in my throat and tightness in my belly.

Old Story	New Story

What if... Consider the worst-case scenario and ask yourself if it's likely to happen or just fear. Then reframe each problem/challenge into an opportunity.

Evaluate the Risks & Rewards of Action/Inaction

Risk	Reward

Action	Inaction

If what you want is necessary and important, decide to act right now.

If not, let it go. Unless or until it becomes important, it's not and is an energy drain.

Ask and Commit

What **one thing** can you do to change/let go of/advance that will make you happier and bring you peace and joy?

Thoughts:

Feelings:

Potential Actions:

Finally, write a Positive Affirmation/Mantra that will help support and manifest your ideal new story.

Routines and Habits

I have daily appointment at 6:30 a.m. every day on my calendar: Write 500 words or for one hour. I rarely miss a day, and if I do, I don't beat myself up about it.

Our routines become habits. This is nothing new. There are many great books about breaking bad habits and creating good ones. Two of my favorites are *Atomic Habits* by James Clear and *The Power of Habit* by Charles Duhigg. Each author offers stories, insights, and strategies for building better habits, and to let go of the ones that don't serve us well.

While new information and insights may be helpful to learn, when it comes to routines and habits, knowing a strategy won't change anything. If we want something to change, we must not only *learn* how to do something different, but we must also *do* it.

That means swallowing our insecurities about failure, success, rejection, and the dreaded imposter syndrome. It means we must risk our ego and pride and ask for help then help ourselves.

Until then, we will continue doing what we've been doing and getting what we've got. If you're OK with that, fine. If not, I implore you to find the courage and guts to take a chance on yourself and start practicing some of the many things you've been thinking about and craving for far too long.

It's dinner time. The food is on the table, time to fill your plate and eat.

Room to Write, Reflect & Respond

Consider these questions/prompts when and where they're appropriate:

What does this prompt stir in you?

Positive	Negative

What resistance, if any do you feel and where?

For example: Before I speak or make cold-calls I feel a knot in my throat and tightness in my belly.

Old Story	New Story

What if... Consider the worst-case scenario and ask yourself if it's likely to happen or just fear. Then reframe each problem/challenge into an opportunity.

Evaluate the Risks & Rewards of Action/Inaction

Risk	Reward

Action	Inaction

If what you want is necessary and important, decide to act right now.

If not, let it go. Unless or until it becomes important, it's not and is an energy drain.

Ask and Commit

What **one thing** can you do to change/let go of/advance that will make you happier and bring you peace and joy?

Thoughts:

Feelings:

Potential Actions:

Finally, write a Positive Affirmation/Mantra that will help support and manifest your ideal new story.

Practice. Practice. Practice.

Besides your age, weight, wrinkles, or other mental and physical traits, *nothing significant in your life will ever change without effort.*

Any meaningful and lasting transformation requires practice. This includes new skills or habits you want to develop. In addition to a disciplined practice routine, you must also be willing to fail. And driven to keep at it until you are competent, then continue until you master that new habit or skill. This is not rocket science. So why do we tend to complicate it?

I don't know, exactly.

But I do know and so do you, that practice and getting your hands dirty are necessary steps to any worthy accomplishment.

And yet, so many of us continue to take short cuts or expect that we can coast or get by on half-assed efforts. Or the other extreme—we drive ourselves so hard and fast that we burn out because we want everything yesterday. There are no magic pills or short cuts. Mastery of anything requires practice, failure, effort, and patience. Lots of patience.

Life is a marathon not a sprint. The joy of abundant living happens as we practice. As we fall down and scrape our elbows. When that happens, rub some dirt in it. Then get back up and keep at it until you succeed. Also, realize that success is not a destination. It is what happens *as you practice*.

Room to Write, Reflect & Respond

Consider these questions/prompts when and where they're appropriate:

What does this prompt stir in you?

Positive	Negative

What resistance, if any do you feel and where?

For example: Before I speak or make cold-calls I feel a knot in my throat and tightness in my belly.

Old Story	New Story

What if... Consider the worst-case scenario and ask yourself if it's likely to happen or just fear. Then reframe each problem/challenge into an opportunity.

Evaluate the Risks & Rewards of Action/Inaction

Risk	Reward

Action	Inaction

If what you want is necessary and important, decide to act right now.
If not, let it go. Unless or until it becomes important, it's not and is an energy drain.

Ask and Commit
What **one thing** can you do to change/let go of/advance that will make you happier and bring you peace and joy?

Thoughts:

Feelings:

Potential Actions:

Finally, write a Positive Affirmation/Mantra that will help support and manifest your ideal new story.

Dare to Be Great

Do you want to be great at something? Or maybe just really, really good? Or, at the very least, better today than you were yesterday? If so, keep reading.

In the last chapter, we talked about practice. In this one, we dare to be great.

What does that mean?

Greatness is a state of mastery and unflinching confidence and expertise for a given skill, state of being, or state of mind. Greatness is accomplished through mastery. Of incremental growth from spaced repetition (practice) over time. Greatness is a result of commitment, effort, and diligence.

Those we consider great are experts in some area of their lives. **Experts *know* because they have done.** A common character trait of those who are or aspire to be great is a *clear and convicting motive*—a white-hot why. They are also bold enough to keep going despite internal or external obstacles. Those determined to become great love the chase. They embrace and do not cower when faced with challenges. In fact, they welcome them because they know challenges make them stronger, more decisive, and more confident as they resolve to adapt and overcome.

Greatness in any area is attainable for those who dare to achieve it, and who find the courage within to press on in the face of real or perceived limitations and obstacles.

Greatness is achieved for those who say *I can*, not *I can't*. Dismiss the fear-filled voices and critics in your head—those that say they can't or that you are not worthy, capable, courageous enough to be great—with this one bold statement:

"Watch me!"

Room to Write, Reflect & Respond

Consider these questions/prompts when and where they're appropriate:

What does this prompt stir in you?

Positive	Negative

What resistance, if any do you feel and where?

For example: Before I speak or make cold-calls I feel a knot in my throat and tightness in my belly.

Old Story	New Story

What if… Consider the worst-case scenario and ask yourself if it's likely to happen or just fear. Then reframe each problem/challenge into an opportunity.

Evaluate the Risks & Rewards of Action/Inaction

Risk	Reward

Action	Inaction

If what you want is necessary and important, decide to act right now.
If not, let it go. Unless or until it becomes important, it's not and is an energy drain.

Ask and Commit

What **one thing** can you do to change/let go of/advance that will make you happier and bring you peace and joy?

Thoughts:

Feelings:

Potential Actions:

Finally, write a Positive Affirmation/Mantra that will help support and manifest your ideal new story.

Be Yourself, Always

Nobody else is you. So why would you want to be anyone other than who you were created to be?

OK, so maybe you have shortcomings, inadequacies, fears, and a hundred and one excuses about who you think you should be or who you want to be or what you should do with the rest of your life. Those thoughts are normal. And some of those ideas/beliefs may be true, but they may also be holding you back.

What do I mean?

I believe every single one of us has been born with a specific purpose for our lives. It is our responsibility to ask, seek, and embrace that purpose when we find it. But when we become so absorbed with negative thoughts about what we are not or what we don't have, we basically lock ourselves into a prison of limitation, never fully realizing our God-given potential and purpose.

Today is a great day to grab the keys around your waist, slide them into the cell door and set yourself free.

Be yourself.

Not what your parents want you to be. Not what your spiritual leader says you should be. Not what you think others want you to be. None of that. Just be you.

This is the day to take a long walk along a coastal path. To find a meadow teeming with lupine where you can sit in quiet contemplation while casting your gaze beyond the horizon of the sea to a world of possibility, all while asking yourself who you are and who you really want to be.

This is a gut check moment. Be honest and open to whatever inspiration the universe plants in your heart, mind, and soul. Then, as a toddler learning to walk, get back on your feet and step onto the path that leads you back to where you are, saying with a smile, "I am free to be me."

And say it again, louder, **"I am free to be me."**

Keep saying it until you feel it pulsating through your flesh and bones. When you arrive there, you will not only believe it to be so—you will also know.

Room to Write, Reflect & Respond

Consider these questions/prompts when and where they're appropriate:

What does this prompt stir in you?

Positive	Negative

What resistance, if any do you feel and where?

For example: Before I speak or make cold-calls I feel a knot in my throat and tightness in my belly.

Old Story	New Story

What if... Consider the worst-case scenario and ask yourself if it's likely to happen or just fear. Then reframe each problem/challenge into an opportunity.

Evaluate the Risks & Rewards of Action/Inaction

Risk	Reward

Action	Inaction

If what you want is necessary and important, decide to act right now.

If not, let it go. Unless or until it becomes important, it's not and is an energy drain.

Ask and Commit

What **one thing** can you do to change/let go of/advance that will make you happier and bring you peace and joy?

Thoughts:

Feelings:

Potential Actions:

Finally, write a Positive Affirmation/Mantra that will help support and manifest your ideal new story.

Embrace Fear, Change, and the Unknown, and Do it Anyway

A white-knuckled grip is not the solution to overcome fear of change and the unknown. Ask anyone in recovery and they will quickly tell you that selfishness, self-will, and self-centered fear are the roots of their problem, not booze or drugs.

Whether you suffer from addiction or not, knowing this does not make a damn bit of difference if you continue to implement strategies that don't work.

But so many of us are creatures of habit, gripping tightly the steering wheel of our lives, thinking that we are in total control; that everything in our lives is for and about us.

Really?

I used to think that too until a friend said "It sounds like you're pretending to be God. If you think you are that powerful," he continued, "when's the last time you stopped a wave?"

So, what needs to change and why should we embrace it? Maybe you don't. But if there are areas of your life that are causing your pain or not fulfilling your soul, you may want to look closer at what is in your way. My guess is you won't have to look too deeply. In all probability the chances are it's your refusal or resistance to change. And beneath that is fear. So, the solution starts with courage. Courage to want to change.

Then comes willingness, followed by a plan. So, what's your plan? To stay where you are, stuck? Or find the inner warrior and enough courage to want to change. To start to get better?

Yes, we can make different plans, decisions, and do something new, but most of us won't or don't because we are too afraid of that which we cannot taste, touch, feel, or see.

Some of the greatest accomplishments and joys in my own life have happened when I showed up, did something new, and got the hell out of my own way; when I allowed the universe to work in and through me and others, to create something far more magnificent than I could have imagined or produced solely by individual effort.

For example, many years ago I went on a mission trip to an orphanage in Mexico with members of a church I was attending at the time. We were there to serve. My task with the pastor's daughter was to renovate a trailer for a doctor who would be moving in to serve the community, including the many orphans who lived and went to school there.

The work was exhausting—cleaning, painting, and installing towel bars and paper towel holders—but also gratifying. This may seem mundane to some, but for me it felt like I was doing something important, God's work. By giving to someone else who would also be giving their time, compassion, and expertise to those in need, it made the long working hours with little sleep seem more important and bigger than my own selfish interests. I don't know who the doctor was or how many kids they may have helped in their time of service at the orphanage. I don't need to. The point is, for that week, I showed up willing to serve someone I didn't know because that was why I was there. I had a clear purpose even though I didn't know the details.

And so it is in our everyday lives. In our families, at work to strangers in the check-out line at the grocery store. With whomever we meet, wherever we go. **If we show up ready to serve or listen, we can do no wrong.** We don't need all the details. Sometimes trusting our gut, skills, and instincts are more than we will ever need.

We didn't paint the place perfect. We didn't have the right tools, or even the right brackets to mount the towel bars. We didn't know what our work assignment would be. It didn't matter. Because we were willing to show up and serve and embrace the unknown, we did the best we could with the tools, resources, and skills we had.

Isn't that all any of us can do?

Today, is a great day to take a chance by doing what you can, the very best you can, then leave the results up to the universe.

And **as we do, we will know that is enough.**

Room to Write, Reflect & Respond

Consider these questions/prompts when and where they're appropriate:

What does this prompt stir in you?

Positive	Negative

What resistance, if any do you feel and where?

For example: Before I speak or make cold-calls I feel a knot in my throat and tightness in my belly.

Old Story	New Story

What if.:. Consider the worst-case scenario and ask yourself if it's likely to happen or just fear. Then reframe each problem/challenge into an opportunity.

Evaluate the Risks & Rewards of Action/Inaction

Risk	Reward

Action	Inaction

If what you want is necessary and important, decide to act right now.

If not, let it go. Unless or until it becomes important, it's not and is an energy drain.

Ask and Commit

What **one thing** can you do to change/let go of/advance that will make you happier and bring you peace and joy?

Thoughts:

Feelings:

Potential Actions:

Finally, write a Positive Affirmation/Mantra that will help support and manifest your ideal new story.

Out with the Old to Make Room for the New

Most of us have too much junk in our heads—fears, worries, doubts, appointments, obligations, deadlines, etc. Like an overstuffed garage, our minds become filled with hundreds of things we no longer use or need, like broken TVs, or outdated computers, or old clothes that no longer fit, and scores of other things that have outlived their usefulness. As a result, we feel weighed down. Unmotivated, if not downright lazy. Worse, we keep wasting time thinking and worrying about things we can't control, which only adds more stress.

To feel better about ourselves we must become willing to let go of some of our habits and old ways of thinking. To stop believing the lies that we aren't good enough. That we have "always been this way" and that "we can never change."

These statements are lies. Lies we continue to say to ourselves and actually believe, which therefore become self-fulfilling prophecies, a negative feedback loop for our own perpetual doom. How self-destructive!

But there are a few simple things we can do to disrupt the pattern of procrastination, worry, and feeling crappy about ourselves because we're not doing the things we think of, dream of, or want to do.

Before we start, we must ask ourselves a few questions, starting with *what do we keep and what do we get rid of?* It's time for a mental garage sale, a few trips to Goodwill, or a dump run. Time to get rid of old habits which are not fulfilling us so we can make room for the creative energy necessary to pursue what we really want and to clarify why we want it.

What does getting rid of old stuff have to do with finding your why, purpose, or calling?

If your garage is like mine, there's still way too much crap in it. Maybe it's still a cluttered mess, because you cannot yet decide what to keep, donate, or discard. So, like me, you likely procrastinate.

My physical garage is a wreck, again. We remodeled two years ago and have yet to do what I suggested above for our mental house cleaning. Bins marked "keep" and "donate" remain stacked in our garage. Plus, there's a dump pile five feet high in our backyard.

It's normal to put off things that are not a priority. Cleaning the garage or doing a dump run are not priorities right now. So, I guess you can say this is prioritization by planned procrastination which is different than denial, avoidance, or pure procrastination which are typically driven by uncertainty, laziness, or some type of fear.

However, when our motives are clear and our desire or need is great enough, most of us will get into action to do what needs to be done. When they aren't, we won't.

The truth is, most of us procrastinate because we are not clear about what we want or what the perceived benefits are. What's more, we also have a confidence and belief problem: We are not sure if the effort we invest will produce the results we want, of our ability, or if we have the drive to even get started.

Instead, we keep adding to the crap that's already in our mental garage. And soon we can't find anything when we need it. We are not motivated to clean it, so the garages (mental and physical) remain cluttered. We remain scattered, unsure, blocked, and that impedes our ability to feel confident or productive.

Hopefully we will wake up one day and say, "today's the day." Then make a decision to make a trip to the dump; to clear out our physical and or mental garage.

Is today your day to make a dump run?

Room to Write, Reflect & Respond

Consider these questions/prompts when and where they're appropriate:

What does this prompt stir in you?

Positive	Negative

What resistance, if any do you feel and where?

For example: Before I speak or make cold-calls I feel a knot in my throat and tightness in my belly.

Old Story	New Story

What if… Consider the worst-case scenario and ask yourself if it's likely to happen or just fear. Then reframe each problem/challenge into an opportunity.

Evaluate the Risks & Rewards of Action/Inaction

Risk	Reward

Action	Inaction

If what you want is necessary and important, decide to act right now.

If not, let it go. Unless or until it becomes important, it's not and is an energy drain.

Ask and Commit

What **one thing** can you do to change/let go of/advance that will make you happier and bring you peace and joy?

Thoughts:

Feelings:

Potential Actions:

Finally, write a Positive Affirmation/Mantra that will help support and manifest your ideal new story.

Change is Not as Scary as You May Think

For those who are in the early stages of learning about the power of personal growth and developing a practice of perpetual self-improvement, know this—**we all struggle with confidence.** And most of us are procrastinators, especially when facing new things. A word of advice, when you feel the butterflies about something that makes you feel anxious or unsure, even terrified, **muster the courage you already have within and do it anyway.**

That is how you will become more confident.

Don't worry about making a mistake or doing things perfect. **We all make mistakes, and we all fall down.** *Those who become better, even great, are the ones who keep getting back up again.* ***Those who win, never give up.***

Room to Write, Reflect & Respond

Consider these questions/prompts when and where they're appropriate:

What does this prompt stir in you?

Positive	Negative

What resistance, if any do you feel and where?

For example: Before I speak or make cold-calls I feel a knot in my throat and tightness in my belly.

Old Story	New Story

What if... Consider the worst-case scenario and ask yourself if it's likely to happen or just fear. Then reframe each problem/challenge into an opportunity.

Evaluate the Risks & Rewards of Action/Inaction

Risk	Reward

Action	Inaction

If what you want is necessary and important, decide to act right now.

If not, let it go. Unless or until it becomes important, it's not and is an energy drain.

Ask and Commit

What **one thing** can you do to change/let go of/advance that will make you happier and bring you peace and joy?

Thoughts:

Feelings:

Potential Actions:

Finally, write a Positive Affirmation/Mantra that will help support and manifest your ideal new story.

What's Your White-Hot Why?

For any change to take place in our lives, we must have a sincere desire and willingness to become more self-confident. That means facing the truth about what we want and how bad we want it.

It's about becoming bold enough to get started, then zeroing in until you find your white-hot why. Without a compelling reason—a white-hot why—we lack the drive and motivation to sustain the inevitable twists and turns, ups and downs, successes and failures integral to any positive progress or forward momentum. Without a why, we will forever remain stuck, possibly so afraid of failing that we never find the guts to start.

We must also accept failure as a key ingredient to success.

Why?

Because our default decision making process is rooted in what won't work or what's missing. To zero in on our why and create better patterns of success (however you define it), we must honestly look at and address these three primary blocks:

1. Unclear motives
2. Unrealistic expectations
3. Impatience

To face our fears and put in the effort necessary to move closer to the person we want to be or what we want to change we must first find our white-hot why. Without it we will not be motivated enough to persist.

Each of us have different reasons for wanting or needing to change. For many, it's pain or fear of loss or missing out. For others, pleasure is a key driver to moving us in a new direction, hopefully positive.

As I said earlier, **the solution is simple: when our motives are clear and our desire or need is great enough, most of us will get into action to do what needs to be done.**

As we clarify what we want and set realistic expectations about what it will take to get it, we understand that we must get to work—get busy with it. We must also learn to relinquish our desire to control conditions and outcomes by letting go of the results. That requires *discipline, practice, and patience.*

You know what each of these are and, if you're honest with yourself, also know where and what you may be able to do to improve in each of these three areas. But remember, without a top of mind white-hot why, you likely won't have the energy to drive the results you want or new state you are trying to create.

Into Action/Practice/Get Busy With It:

Take a few moments to journal about the things that motivate you. Ask yourself, what really matters to me? What do I want? What am I willing to do to get it? What will it mean to me to get that, be that, do that, or change that, whatever "that" is? Now ask, what's in my way? Who can help me? And what can or will I do today to start creating the change I keep saying I want?

Please do this, even if you doubt your ability for follow-through. Especially when the critics start barking again trying to tear you away from change before you even take the first step. Look those liars in their beady eyes and tell them where they can go…. Get mad or sad, but no matter what, take a few minutes to think and write.

Trust me, this is the best investment of your time right now!

Room to Write, Reflect & Respond
Consider these questions/prompts when and where they're appropriate:

What does this prompt stir in you?

Positive	Negative

What resistance, if any do you feel and where?
For example: Before I speak or make cold-calls I feel a knot in my throat and tightness in my belly.

Old Story	New Story

What if... Consider the worst-case scenario and ask yourself if it's likely to happen or just fear. Then reframe each problem/challenge into an opportunity.

Evaluate the Risks & Rewards of Action/Inaction

Risk	Reward

Action	Inaction

If what you want is necessary and important, decide to act right now.

If not, let it go. Unless or until it becomes important, it's not and is an energy drain.

Ask and Commit

What **one thing** can you do to change/let go of/advance that will make you happier and bring you peace and joy?

Thoughts:

Feelings:

Potential Actions:

Finally, write a Positive Affirmation/Mantra that will help support and manifest your ideal new story.

Admit, Accept, and Adapt

Admit:

Unless it will hurt someone else more, admit it when you are wrong, regardless of your title, position or standing.

Some cultures believe it is more important to save face than admit shortcomings. I respect the norms of other cultures, but for me, admitting when I'm wrong reduces stress because I don't have the burden of guilt or shame weighing me down. **If you want to be free of guilt, shame, anger, fear , or resentment, admit your faults and shortcomings.**

Accept:

"It is what it is." One of my former co-workers, often said this whenever she was faced with situations that were challenging or didn't go as planned. She didn't dwell in self-pity. Instead, she learned from the situation and took responsibility for what she could do better next time, then moved on. The key to acceptance is to **develop the habit of having grace with yourself and understanding that mistakes are a normal part of life.**

Adapt:

This is where our mettle is tested. If it's important enough, we will find a way to accomplish what we want. We will adapt out of necessity and because we have a big enough reason to want to—a white-hot why. **If we don't have a big enough want, need, or desire, we won't change. Period.**

What areas of your daily life can you begin to practice admitting where you are wrong? How might it heal relationships? Build respect or trust?

Room to Write, Reflect & Respond

Consider these questions/prompts when and where they're appropriate:

What does this prompt stir in you?

Positive	Negative

What resistance, if any do you feel and where?

For example: Before I speak or make cold-calls I feel a knot in my throat and tightness in my belly.

Old Story	New Story

What if... Consider the worst-case scenario and ask yourself if it's likely to happen or just fear. Then reframe each problem/challenge into an opportunity.

Evaluate the Risks & Rewards of Action/Inaction

Risk	Reward

Action	Inaction

If what you want is necessary and important, decide to act right now.
If not, let it go. Unless or until it becomes important, it's not and is an energy drain.

Ask and Commit
What **one thing** can you do to change/let go of/advance that will make you happier and bring you peace and joy?

Thoughts:

Feelings:

Potential Actions:

Finally, write a Positive Affirmation/Mantra that will help support and manifest your ideal new story.

    What challenges or admissions of your own shortcomings do you need to accept? Can you change deficiencies in your personal skills, knowledge, or behavior? Can you amend processes, strategies, or methodologies applied to your business, career, or leadership roles? What can you do to adapt or improve?

Finding the Courage to Dream and Believe, Again

Do you know of anyone your age who decided to pursue a dream and accomplish it? I know many. People who have gone back to school at forty, fifty, even sixty+ years-old to pursue higher degrees in psychology, interior design, or coaching certification and more. I know others who took the leap to buy a 100-year-old flower shop in their early thirties or open their own restaurant and earn scores of awards as one of the best Italian and fine dining establishments in the county. They had a dream and made it happen. Both are also my clients.

Every day, in every nook and cranny of the globe, people daydream of writing a book, opening their own business, starting a family, buying their first car, or switching jobs or careers. All of us have dreams but unfortunately, they remain unrealized wishes for far too many.

Why? Many reasons, but **the primary blocks are cowardice and a broken or outdated belief system.** There is no assurance of success at the start of any worthy endeavor. That's not how things work. All success requires courage, effort, and belief. If we do not believe we can succeed, we will never muster the courage necessary to get our lazy butts off the sofa to start something.

Every successful person at some point found the courage to start, then figured out what it would take to succeed as they actively pursued their dreams. *As they did, they began to believe.* With each new victory, they began to not only see but also *know* they were well on their way to fulfilling their dreams.

Simply put, if you want to believe again, you need to find the courage to start, be willing to fail, and keep getting back up again until you achieve that which you seek. This takes courage, guts, and determination— an *unwavering commitment and belief that it will all be worth it.*

How bad do you want what you dream about? What are you willing to do to get it? Do you have the guts to take a first step today?

Room to Write, Reflect & Respond

Consider these questions/prompts when and where they're appropriate:

What does this prompt stir in you?

Positive	Negative

What resistance, if any do you feel and where?

For example: Before I speak or make cold-calls I feel a knot in my throat and tightness in my belly.

Old Story	New Story

What if... Consider the worst-case scenario and ask yourself if it's likely to happen or just fear. Then reframe each problem/challenge into an opportunity.

Evaluate the Risks & Rewards of Action/Inaction

Risk	Reward

Action	Inaction

If what you want is necessary and important, decide to act right now.
If not, let it go. Unless or until it becomes important, it's not and is an energy drain.

Ask and Commit
What **one thing** can you do to change/let go of/advance that will make you happier and bring you peace and joy?

Thoughts:

Feelings:

Potential Actions:

Finally, write a Positive Affirmation/Mantra that will help support and manifest your ideal new story.

Dusty Dreams

When I started writing my last book, I flipped through a dusty old notebook from a class I took at a local junior college in my early twenties called *Beyond Goal Setting*.

Inside were pages and pages of goals I'd written decades earlier. As I flipped through the coffee-stained pages, I felt my heart skip a beat realizing that **nearly every single goal I'd written down had come true.**

Writing down your dreams, ambitions, goals, intentions, plans, or whatever you want to call them, is tantamount to manifesting them. They make up the parts of *your action plan* to write the next chapters of your life. What type of story will it be? What will happen? Will it have a happy ending? What obstacles will you face? How will you overcome them? You won't know until you dive in. And that's what makes this all so exciting.

The most important and powerful piece of advice I can offer you is this:

Write down your goals.

Even if you never read them again, something magical happens by this simple act—you set the wheels of manifestation in motion. The universe, your mind, and other unseen forces begin to align and collaborate, creating a clearer path toward their accomplishment, providing you with ample opportunities to take action toward achievement.

The simple process of writing down that which you want to be, have, or do will change your life.

Yes, dusty dreams can come true. **It's all up to you.**

Again, I must ask, how bad do you want to accomplish them and improve the quality of your life?

Room to Write, Reflect & Respond

Consider these questions/prompts when and where they're appropriate:

What does this prompt stir in you?

Positive	Negative

What resistance, if any do you feel and where?

For example: Before I speak or make cold-calls I feel a knot in my throat and tightness in my belly.

Old Story	New Story

What if... Consider the worst-case scenario and ask yourself if it's likely to happen or just fear. Then reframe each problem/challenge into an opportunity.

Evaluate the Risks & Rewards of Action/Inaction

Risk	Reward

Action	Inaction

If what you want is necessary and important, decide to act right now.

If not, let it go. Unless or until it becomes important, it's not and is an energy drain.

Ask and Commit

What **one thing** can you do to change/let go of/advance that will make you happier and bring you peace and joy?

Thoughts:

Feelings:

Potential Actions:

Finally, write a Positive Affirmation/Mantra that will help support and manifest your ideal new story.

Creating Compound Confidence is a Process

In *Atomic Habits*, James Clear shares a simple yet, as he argues, highly effective strategy called habit stacking. I agree with the principle even if it is called various things. In principle, success begets success. As long as we maintain a discipline of perpetual continuous self-improvement or innovation (having the discipline to continue doing the things we did to win)—healthy habits—we, our businesses, and those we serve will continue to improve.

But there's a catch: if/when we stop the new routines, often at the first misstep or "failure" (before they become a healthy habit), we quickly lose any confidence or momentum we had previously built. When that happens, it frequently takes way more effort and energy than we can muster to overcome our negative emotions and baggage by not living up to our full potential. As a result, we may feel like failures.

Therefore, if we want to change or improve, we must pay attention to what we did right and adjust what didn't work. We must keep stacking our wins as they come.

This concept or premise is not necessarily unique. As you continue to become more adept in one area of your life, add to your list of wins and successes. This way you can continue to increase your confidence and belief in yourself, plus increase your skill and ability on your way to accomplishing what you want.

I refer to this as *compound confidence*: building on your successes and wins to create positive forward momentum.

Compound confidence is a mindset in which confidence grows exponentially upon each previous success. It is created by doing, practicing, and/or completing an ongoing series of incremental steps toward a desired outcome.

How to leverage your wins:

It's not uncommon to feel more confident when approaching the next problem, goal, or opportunity after a victory. As a salesperson for the past three decades, I have learned the best time to make another sales call or find the guts to cold call a new prospect is right after I've closed a sale.

Why?

Because I have more energy, I am buzzing with confidence, which emanates in the tone of my voice, my body language, and my being. It works, as long as I remember to not become cocky or arrogant, and when I follow the same process, mindset, and approach I used to win a previous sale: to ask better questions and offer to help another client increase *their* business.

As you win, I encourage you to write your successes in a notebook or folder labeled *confidence bank*. Deposit often when things are going well. Inevitably you will need to draw upon previous wins whenever you get frustrated or feel like an imposter. **Keep your account flush and don't let it get overdrawn.**

As I mentioned several times before, starting any new endeavor feels awkward and uncomfortable at first. Don't fight it. Instead, *accept it, expect it, and embrace it.*

Life and our personal growth are not races to be won. They are ever evolving states of awakening and enlightenment. Of better understanding who we are and what our true purpose is as we mature.

New habits take time to develop. Therefore, you will need to be patient and kind to yourself as you progress. You will make mistakes, we all do. But the difference between those who exude self-confidence and those who don't is usually a result of three controllable factors: *practice, discipline, and repetition.*

Remember this: *Confidence is a byproduct of vulnerability, courage, and action.*

Why these?

Because they all require change, and most people don't readily embrace change. We are creatures of habit. We like control and predictability, and we have a hard time accepting when things don't work out according to our plans. Your success in any endeavor is and will be predicated on developing a daily habit of thinking about the changes you want to make and writing down your goals. As you do, you will begin to realign your attention toward your intentions or ambitions. You will begin to make the mental shift from *"I can't"* to *"How can I?"*

Into Action/Practice/Get Busy With It:

Right now, I want you to focus on **one specific problem or opportunity**: on what you want to change, get rid of, or accomplish.

Be as general or specific as you wish but resist the urge to think too deeply about each problem you want to solve or goal you want to achieve. For right now, just write them down.

You'll be amazed at how liberating it feels to actually get started. It's like dropping a hundred-pound sack of rocks off your back, a critical first step to building your self-confidence.

Here are a few examples:
- I want to make more money than month.
- I want to earn x dollars per year.
- I want to get out of debt.
- I want to be more confident in social situations.
- I want to lose x pounds and feel better about who I am and how I look.

"If you keep doing what you've been doing, you'll keep getting what you've got."

Courage and confidence are built on the battlefield of life. Our greatest battles are fought within—the internal ones we fight everyday between our ears. If you want to break free, it stands to reason that we'll have to do a few things differently and a few different things, right? That's awesome, because even if we won't admit it, don't most of us secretly want to be unique? Successful? Loved? To belong?

Are you ready to start developing some new habits to become more self-confident?

Well, here's your chance.

What are you waiting for?

Time to get busy with it.

Room to Write, Reflect & Respond

Consider these questions/prompts when and where they're appropriate:

What does this prompt stir in you?

Positive	Negative

What resistance, if any do you feel and where?

For example: Before I speak or make cold-calls I feel a knot in my throat and tightness in my belly.

Old Story	New Story

What if... Consider the worst-case scenario and ask yourself if it's likely to happen or just fear. Then reframe each problem/challenge into an opportunity.

Evaluate the Risks & Rewards of Action/Inaction

Risk	Reward

Action	Inaction

If what you want is necessary and important, decide to act right now.
If not, let it go. Unless or until it becomes important, it's not and is an energy drain.

Ask and Commit

What **one thing** can you do to change/let go of/advance that will make you happier and bring you peace and joy?

Thoughts:

Feelings:

Potential Actions:

Finally, write a Positive Affirmation/Mantra that will help support and manifest your ideal new story.

Gratitude, Like Happiness, is a State of Mind

We are responsible for creating our own happiness and states of gratitude.

Happiness is a choice. A decision. One made easier as we begin a daily practice of being grateful.

Into Action/Practice/Get Busy With It:
Let's pause for a moment of gratitude. Here. Now.

Take five minutes to write down everything you can think of that you are grateful for. And everything that brings you joy. Read your list, close your eyes, and let the feelings settle in.

After a few minutes, open your eyes and reflect on what came up. What images come to mind? What are your thoughts or feelings? Which make you smile?

As you go about the rest of your day, now and in the future, know that *you can come back to this place of gratitude anywhere, anytime you want to.* All you have to do is **stop. Pause.** And **be grateful.**

Yes, it is that easy.

Room to Write, Reflect & Respond

Consider these questions/prompts when and where they're appropriate:

What does this prompt stir in you?

Positive	Negative

What resistance, if any do you feel and where?

For example: Before I speak or make cold-calls I feel a knot in my throat and tightness in my belly.

Old Story	New Story

What if... Consider the worst-case scenario and ask yourself if it's likely to happen or just fear. Then reframe each problem/challenge into an opportunity.

Evaluate the Risks & Rewards of Action/Inaction

Risk	Reward

Action	Inaction

If what you want is necessary and important, decide to act right now.

If not, let it go. Unless or until it becomes important, it's not and is an energy drain.

Ask and Commit

What **one thing** can you do to change/let go of/advance that will make you happier and bring you peace and joy?

Thoughts:

Feelings:

Potential Actions:

Finally, write a Positive Affirmation/Mantra that will help support and manifest your ideal new story.

Beware of The Comparison Trap

Comparison, self-criticism, worry about others criticizing you, or your own judgment of others, are all poisonous to building healthy self-confidence.

Most of us tend to judge ourselves and our own inadequacies harshly, which keeps us in a state of low self-worth. Not good.

Expecting to be at the same level as someone with more experience and time without proper effort on our part is ridiculous. Unless we are trying to emulate the work habits and experience that has led to others' success, comparing what they have after years of experience is not going to add anything positive to your confidence bank.

Beware of Complacency and Other Confidence Killers

When you succumb to complacency, all the success of your hard work begins to evaporate. Soon you may lose momentum quickly spiraling back to your previous state of equilibrium, or worse, backwards. *If you are going to strive for anything, strive for progress, not perfection.* Do your best always.

Remain mindful of and beware of these confidence killers:
- Judgment
- Comparison
- Pride/Ego
- Overconfidence/Cockiness
- Blame
- Denial
- Victim mentality
- Rejection
- Self-Sabotage
- Feeding your Inner Critics

And leave the results up to the universe. That is how you build confidence: **one bold decision and action at a time.**

Room to Write, Reflect & Respond

Consider these questions/prompts when and where they're appropriate:

What does this prompt stir in you?

Positive	Negative

What resistance, if any do you feel and where?

For example: Before I speak or make cold-calls I feel a knot in my throat and tightness in my belly.

Old Story	New Story

What if... Consider the worst-case scenario and ask yourself if it's likely to happen or just fear. Then reframe each problem/challenge into an opportunity.

Evaluate the Risks & Rewards of Action/Inaction

Risk	Reward

Action	Inaction

If what you want is necessary and important, decide to act right now.

If not, let it go. Unless or until it becomes important, it's not and is an energy drain.

Ask and Commit

What **one thing** can you do to change/let go of/advance that will make you happier and bring you peace and joy?

Thoughts:

Feelings:

Potential Actions:

Finally, write a Positive Affirmation/Mantra that will help support and manifest your ideal new story.

Finding Our Why

"He who has a why to live for can bear almost any how."
Friedrich Nietzsche.

Three keys to living a meaningful and purposeful life are: *Belief, willingness, and love.* They are integral to helping you clarify and discover your *motives, purpose, and drive.* The goal here is to help you find and clarify your why so you can become more confident and thrive in all areas of your life: *finances, relationships, career, mental, physical, emotional, spiritual, etc.* You may discover as we continue that our why is dynamic and fluid. Your goals are not always an end result or destination. That would make them transactional. The lasting and, in my opinion, far greater rewards lie in our pursuit of why with a mindset and objective of transformation and *becoming* rather than mere achievement, acquisition, and accomplishment.

Our why is our raison de étre. Our reason for being. For living. Our purpose. Our calling.

When we find and discover a purpose and motive that is greater than our own selfish wants, needs, or desires, something magical happens—the universe reveals endless opportunities for fulfillment. It paves the way for us to practice, grow, and serve. Our mission is to be vigilant and courageous enough to answer the call when prompted.

Conversely, when we choose to remain in a state of fear, feeling like a victim of circumstance, we further exacerbate and perpetuate a state of dissatisfaction or despair. Who wants that? Not me.

Today, I encourage you to consider the five most important things and values—big rocks—in your life and begin to focus 80% of your time, energy, and attention into enhancing them. As you identify them ask yourself several times throughout the day, is this moving me closer to X? If not, why? Honestly ask yourself what different decision or action should I take to get back on track?

No guilt. No shame. Just incremental improvement and practice until this becomes a habit. As you do, you will soon discover that decisions become easier. Your value system will become a new barometer. Your life will become simpler, less stressful.

A few words of caution: you must also learn how to give yourself grace and allow room for mistakes. Practice letting go of mistakes. Learn from them and vow to do better next time. Don't fall into the victim and self-pity guilt trap. **Own your life.** Take responsibility for the person you want to be and let each victory be one more deposit into your confidence bank. Soon you will discover that life is much more meaningful when you uncover your why. It also becomes richer, more satisfying, and more fulfilling as you *stay on a path of progress, not perfection.*

Room to Write, Reflect & Respond
Consider these questions/prompts when and where they're appropriate:

What does this prompt stir in you?

Positive	Negative

What resistance, if any do you feel and where?
For example: Before I speak or make cold-calls I feel a knot in my throat and tightness in my belly.

Old Story	New Story

What if... Consider the worst-case scenario and ask yourself if it's likely to happen or just fear. Then reframe each problem/challenge into an opportunity.

Evaluate the Risks & Rewards of Action/Inaction

Risk	Reward

Action	Inaction

If what you want is necessary and important, decide to act right now.
If not, let it go. Unless or until it becomes important, it's not and is an energy drain.

Ask and Commit

What **one thing** can you do to change/let go of/advance that will make you happier and bring you peace and joy?

Thoughts:

Feelings:

Potential Actions:

Finally, write a Positive Affirmation/Mantra that will help support and manifest your ideal new story.

Big Rocks First

What are the big rocks you chose in the last chapter? What or who do you value most? Are the valued things and people in your life given the priority they deserve? In other words, are your purported values aligned with where you invest most of your time, money, and energy? If not, why? What is in your way? And what can you do to change it? To get back on track?

These questions are deep and personal. As such, I am just going to leave them here for you to ponder. Whatever you come up with, they represent your reality in this moment.

Your motives and goals will shift over time. That is perfectly normal. But the big rocks are the pillars and foundational values you believe and live by, and they rarely change. They are solid and, when not given the attention and priority they deserve, we tend to feel off balance, stressed, and uptight.

In my case I know when my priorities are out of whack. Usually when I am trying to control people, places, and things to suit my needs. When I am selfish, self-centered, and more concerned about accomplishment or looking good on the outside. For me this is dangerous. But as soon as I refocus my energy and attention on a power greater than myself, and serving others, I return to a state of gratitude and feel whole again. Life returns to an easy, stress-free pace. In other words when I am stuck in self-will, my days are shitty. As soon as I take my eyes off myself and onto God or others, my days become fun again.

To cut to the chase, my biggest rocks in order of priority are my higher power, sobriety, family, friends, and my vocation. Woven into each are character traits which hold equal if not greater value than the other big rocks. These are: *honesty, humility, courage, love, focus, forgiveness, willingness, effort, commitment, and conviction.*

Wherever you currently land on the mental, physical, emotional, or spiritual collective continuum, I encourage you to invest the time to **clearly identify what the big rocks and values are in *your* life and to nurture them in all you do.**

A promise: As we explore and integrate these "big rocks" into our lives, everything will seem smoother. We will not be as stressed or spun, especially if we have some sense of spirituality or relationship with a power greater than ourselves. With clear values, meaning, and purpose (big rocks) behind all we do at home, work, and in our relationships, we tend to feel a greater sense of inner peace and direction.

If you are not clear what your big rocks are, I urge you to spend considerable time over the next several weeks until you do. It will be one of the healthiest things you can do for the rest of your life.

To help you get started, let's see what values (your big rocks) emerge as you consider and answer the five questions in the prompt below.

Into Action/Practice/Get Busy With It:
Today is a great day for contemplation. Consider and ask yourself these five important questions:

1. What do I think I really want?
2. What am I good at?
3. What is really holding me back?
4. Why do I want it? / What are my motives?
5. What am I willing to do to get it?

I encourage you to grab a journal or notebook and spend fifteen to thirty minutes jotting down your initial thoughts, feelings, experiences, successes, and failures—anything you believe is important to help you succeed. Don't overthink any of your responses, just write as much as you can.

The purpose of this exercise is to explore and perhaps begin to clarify what is important to you and what skills and talents you already have.

Note: There are no right or wrong answers. I urge you to get started now. Doing so will set the stage for the rest of your day and you will likely feel less stressed and more confident to face whatever challenges come your way

For now, do as much as you can in the time allotted. This critical activity will help you begin to develop a habit of introspection and start aligning what you want with what you value as we discussed earlier.

I encourage you to revisit these questions as often as you like and to add more detail and clarification. As you do, *you will likely begin to see a natural shift toward feeling better about the direction your life is moving because you have identified and honor your big rocks and have invested the time to take control of your own destiny.*

Room to Write, Reflect & Respond

Consider these questions/prompts when and where they're appropriate:

What does this prompt stir in you?

Positive	Negative

What resistance, if any do you feel and where?

For example: Before I speak or make cold-calls I feel a knot in my throat and tightness in my belly.

Old Story	New Story

What if... Consider the worst-case scenario and ask yourself if it's likely to happen or just fear. Then reframe each problem/challenge into an opportunity.

Evaluate the Risks & Rewards of Action/Inaction

Risk	Reward

Action	Inaction

If what you want is necessary and important, decide to act right now.

If not, let it go. Unless or until it becomes important, it's not and is an energy drain.

Ask and Commit

What **one thing** can you do to change/let go of/advance that will make you happier and bring you peace and joy?

Thoughts:

Feelings:

Potential Actions:

Finally, write a Positive Affirmation/Mantra that will help support and manifest your ideal new story.

A River of Ambitions

The following is an excerpt from *Ten Seconds of Boldness* you may find valuable.

A River of Ambitions

You and your dreams are worth the effort it will take to accomplish the change you seek. But you have to invest some time figuring out what that means to you. Without a clear direction and a reason why, all your efforts will be wasted. The temptation to give up before you are halfway there will be too great and you will forever remain where you are.

All greatness requires boldness, bravery, and courage at some point. It's the price of admission. The sooner you understand and accept that fact and start becoming more daring, the faster and sooner you will build the confidence to become the person you want to be and do the things that until now have likely seemed out of reach.

Another way to approach each of the five important questions is to think of them as a river of ambitions and you are in a kayak with a paddle. Somedays your thoughts, dreams, goals, and challenges will be clear, flowing at a steady pace like a river's surface on a calm day; other days may feel like you're in a raging torrent, with white-water rapids, struggling to survive as you twist and turn around huge boulders. This can be exhilarating or frightening or both depending on your experience navigating the ever-changing rivers of life. Whatever your response, don't fight the river. The boulders will always be there. The river never stops. But your course may change depending on the conditions of the day. That is perfectly normal and smart.

Don't fear obstacles or setbacks. Expect them. Be prepared and learn to deal with them. I will admit when it comes to other people's problems it is always easier to offer advice or wisdom. But when the time comes to take an honest look within to thoroughly examine our own thoughts, actions, and behaviors we crumble.

For some, the introspection necessary to overcome years of bad habits and negative ways of thinking will seem too painful. It's not.

Like cleaning out an overcrowded garage, we need to start with one cabinet or corner at a time. For our purposes, that one thing is the courage to tackle each problem in turn.

This will build a track record of success and help you become more self-confident.

Room to Write, Reflect & Respond

Consider these questions/prompts when and where they're appropriate:

What does this prompt stir in you?

Positive	Negative

What resistance, if any do you feel and where?

For example: Before I speak or make cold-calls I feel a knot in my throat and tightness in my belly.

Old Story	New Story

What if... Consider the worst-case scenario and ask yourself if it's likely to happen or just fear. Then reframe each problem/challenge into an opportunity.

Evaluate the Risks & Rewards of Action/Inaction

Risk	Reward

Action	Inaction

If what you want is necessary and important, decide to act right now.

If not, let it go. Unless or until it becomes important, it's not and is an energy drain.

Ask and Commit

What **one thing** can you do to change/let go of/advance that will make you happier and bring you peace and joy?

Thoughts:

Feelings:

Potential Actions:

Finally, write a Positive Affirmation/Mantra that will help support and manifest your ideal new story.

Upstream

Resistance is good and bad. It protects us from disease, and it builds muscle, protecting us and making us stronger. On the flip side, resistance in the form of mental or emotional obstacles, such as fear, denial, self-doubt, etc., can cripple us, if we let it.

As with happiness, resistance to a perceived problem is largely a habit. And a bad one. A choice. When something presents itself as a potential obstacle such as an unfamiliar situation or something that we want to do but don't know that we can or can't do, we typically respond with avoidance or resistance; fear.

Succumbing to our fears will not move us closer to being braver or bolder. Our fears will win every time we give in to them, leaving us to feel inadequate, less worthy, and less confident.

The way to overcome the paralyzing emotions often rooted in fear is to jump in our kayak and paddle upstream. Against the rivers of doubt, fear, insecurity, inadequacy. Against the waves of rejection, and feelings of being inept because we've never been in a kayak on a river before.

When we choose to get in that wobbly kayak and paddle, an amazing thing happens. We feel it in our gut. We begin to ease our way upstream, gaining confidence, building momentum, gliding atop the river, one paddle stroke at a time.

But where are we padding to? What are we paddling from? Those are the questions you get to decide.

Into Action/Practice/Get Busy With It:
Review the five questions you answered earlier, then make some decisions.

Five Important Questions to Ask Yourself:
1. What do I think I really want?
2. What am I good at?
3. What is really holding me back?
4. Why do I want it? / What are my motives?
5. What am I willing to do to get it?

Invest time to think about where you want to go and why you want to go there. This is a practice that will increase your resistance against all the negative thoughts that want to wash you out to sea. Each day you paddle you grow stronger and more confident.

Paddling against the current requires far more energy and effort than floating downstream, but often the greatest rewards are found upstream not downstream.

The next bold step is to start making some decisions about what you are going to do or not do about each of your ongoing, ever-changing list of questions.

Here's a short prompt to get you started.

Decision Making Practice
1. Decide to identify and admit there's a problem
2. Decide what you want and what you're going to do about it.
3. Decide to find out why you want it.
4. Decide what you're willing to do to get it.
5. Decide to get into action and to never give up.

Room to Write, Reflect & Respond

Consider these questions/prompts when and where they're appropriate:

What does this prompt stir in you?

Positive	Negative

What resistance, if any do you feel and where?

For example: Before I speak or make cold-calls I feel a knot in my throat and tightness in my belly.

Old Story	New Story

What if... Consider the worst-case scenario and ask yourself if it's likely to happen or just fear. Then reframe each problem/challenge into an opportunity.

Evaluate the Risks & Rewards of Action/Inaction

Risk	Reward

Action	Inaction

If what you want is necessary and important, decide to act right now.

If not, let it go. Unless or until it becomes important, it's not and is an energy drain.

Ask and Commit

What **one thing** can you do to change/let go of/advance that will make you happier and bring you peace and joy?

Thoughts:

Feelings:

Potential Actions:

Finally, write a Positive Affirmation/Mantra that will help support and manifest your ideal new story.

Go with the Flow

Going with the flow may sound completely paradoxical to what we discussed in the previous section about resistance and our need to paddle upstream. It's not. Life is perpetual motion. As long as we are breathing and our heart is beating, our blood continues to circulate.

Expansion and contraction of the heart makes that possible. In other words**, life is a balance between beats of exertion and rest.**

There will be times when we do need to be in charge, furiously paddling to get to a destination upriver. Other times we need to float, go with the flow. This is equally vital for our health.

It's recharging and refreshing to our mind, body, and soul, as we drift downstream watching the blue heron fish along the muddy rivers edge. Watching the cattails bob as red winged blackbirds sing and flit about chasing bugs. Periods of rest are necessary to maintain vitality and keep us in a state of equilibrium.

Today, look for opportunities to refresh and recharge. When they present themselves, or if you chose to intentionally create space to just be present, do so without any attachment to the hundred and one other things that "need" to be done. They can wait. And they will be there when you return.

For now, just put the oar across your lap and float. **Go with the flow.**

Room to Write, Reflect & Respond

Consider these questions/prompts when and where they're appropriate:

What does this prompt stir in you?

Positive	Negative

What resistance, if any do you feel and where?

For example: Before I speak or make cold-calls I feel a knot in my throat and tightness in my belly.

Old Story	New Story

What if... Consider the worst-case scenario and ask yourself if it's likely to happen or just fear. Then reframe each problem/challenge into an opportunity.

Evaluate the Risks & Rewards of Action/Inaction

Risk	Reward

Action	Inaction

If what you want is necessary and important, decide to act right now.

If not, let it go. Unless or until it becomes important, it's not and is an energy drain.

Ask and Commit

What **one thing** can you do to change/let go of/advance that will make you happier and bring you peace and joy?

Thoughts:

Feelings:

Potential Actions:

Finally, write a Positive Affirmation/Mantra that will help support and manifest your ideal new story.

Be Here Now

In his 1971 bestselling book *Be Here Now*, Ram Dass takes the reader on a spiritual journey of awakening and enlightenment. As a conduit of many ancient teachers, his premise is simple but not easy—learn to detach from our ego and become fully aware of the present. This is not a new concept. For millennia, spiritual seekers have sought to find the center. The grounding space free of expectation or obligation. Of just being at one with themselves and their concept of some greater power and energy that transcends space and time. The quest to find inner peace by learning to detach from self, karma, guilt, or shame, or, for some, the perpetual struggle with suffering that we often resist.

The first noble truth of Buddhism is that all life is suffering. A perpetual cycle of samsara or birth, life, death, and rebirth. This cycle is what it is for each and every one of us, whether Buddhist or not. The key to finding serenity and inner peace is to learn to embrace and accept our suffering for what it is trying to teach us.

It's a subtle but transformational shift of our awareness that has the power to change our entire attitude and outlook upon life. Being fully present means completely surrendering our will and our ego, and to awaken to all that is in us, around us, and through us.

As we practice letting go of our attachments to what we think we should be or do or say or have, or how we should behave, we will see how rich and full our lives already are; **in a steady state of being present, alive, alert, and fully awakened where we are, here now.**

Today, breathe. Inhale. Hold. Exhale. Lift your gaze to the horizon and be still.

Now smile, grateful that **you get to do this** *because you are alive!*

Room to Write, Reflect & Respond

Consider these questions/prompts when and where they're appropriate:

What does this prompt stir in you?

Positive	Negative

What resistance, if any do you feel and where?

For example: Before I speak or make cold-calls I feel a knot in my throat and tightness in my belly.

Old Story	New Story

What if... Consider the worst-case scenario and ask yourself if it's likely to happen or just fear. Then reframe each problem/challenge into an opportunity.

Evaluate the Risks & Rewards of Action/Inaction

Risk	Reward

Action	Inaction

If what you want is necessary and important, decide to act right now.
If not, let it go. Unless or until it becomes important, it's not and is an energy drain.

Ask and Commit
What **one thing** can you do to change/let go of/advance that will make you happier and bring you peace and joy?

Thoughts:

Feelings:

Potential Actions:

Finally, write a Positive Affirmation/Mantra that will help support and manifest your ideal new story.

Courage to Change

For decades I have been practicing the Serenity Prayer: "God, grant me the serenity to accept the things I cannot change, the courage to change the things I can, and the wisdom to know the difference."

This prayer saved my life.

In early recovery, the Serenity Prayer became a mantra that helped me face my fears and insecurities. At first it helped me stop thinking about drinking. It has become a multi-functional tool for facing fears or emotionally loaded situations, and building or maintaining healthy relationships with myself, God, and others.

Reciting the prayer silently or aloud and applying its precepts empowers me to focus on finding the courage to change the things I can. That typically means facing some form of fear such as making cold calls for my sales job. Or investing the time to put together a workshop on building belief and self-confidence while simultaneously working on the very things I will teach. Of battling the inner critics that continue to say I am not good enough, that I should be further along in my writing, coaching, and speaking career than I am.

It helps me find the courage to not fall victim to the thinking or overthinking that all too often send me into a tailspin of imposter syndrome, just as I recently dealt with over four months when narrating my audiobook, *Ten Seconds of Boldness,* with professional producers.

We all encounter hundreds of forms of fear and doubt, and daily we must choose whether or not we will believe them and play our victim cards or step up and find the courage within to change.

Finding the courage to change is one of the most exhilarating and life enhancing habits we can develop. The big question is this: will we make bolder decisions and honor our commitments to ourselves and each other—promises to change, grow, improve, or adapt?

Carefully consider these three questions:

Where will you search to find your inner warrior? What will you do when you find it? How will you use your newfound courage to improve the relationships between yourself, God, and others?

Room to Write, Reflect & Respond

Consider these questions/prompts when and where they're appropriate:

What does this prompt stir in you?

Positive	Negative

What resistance, if any do you feel and where?

For example: Before I speak or make cold-calls I feel a knot in my throat and tightness in my belly.

Old Story	New Story

What if... Consider the worst-case scenario and ask yourself if it's likely to happen or just fear. Then reframe each problem/challenge into an opportunity.

Evaluate the Risks & Rewards of Action/Inaction

Risk	Reward

Action	Inaction

If what you want is necessary and important, decide to act right now.
If not, let it go. Unless or until it becomes important, it's not and is an energy drain.

Ask and Commit

What **one thing** can you do to change/let go of/advance that will make you happier and bring you peace and joy?

Thoughts:

Feelings:

Potential Actions:

Finally, write a Positive Affirmation/Mantra that will help support and manifest your ideal new story.

Success is Whatever You Decide it to Be

We've all heard the statement that success is a journey not a destination. But what does that really mean? And do you believe it? If not, why?

We are conditioned from an early age to perform. To equate our value with what we do or how we act. From parents to teachers and later to spouses or bosses, we attach our sense of worth and identity to how others perceive us.

The bigger, more important questions we must ask are about how we perceive ourselves.

How do you measure success?

For example, is success a function of having more money than your friends? Do you compare your car or home or income to others who are of a similar age or in a similar industry? Perhaps you own a business and are constantly fighting to be the best, the top-rated number one business in your field and therefore, the most successful. That can be a trap.

Why?

Because all of these are external measures of worth. They are inadequate measures of our true value.

Is the 62-year-old adult who just got an AA degree from a local junior college a success? Even though he still needs to earn a bachelor's degree in psychology so he can help those who suffer from a myriad of grave emotional or mental disorders? Is he any less successful than those who have already earned the certificate? Already built a thriving practice? No. For him the AA degree is a huge success.

How about the single mom who manages to work two jobs and still go back to school to train to become a massage therapist? Is she successful?

How about you?

Largely fueled by greed, growth, stock price, earnings per share, and quarterly profits, similar traps can be found in the corporate world.

To stakeholders and owners or traders, profit and market share are incredibly important. But corporations and businesses primarily driven by profit and greed often miss the larger, more lasting prize: building a stickier and healthier relationship with their customers and the employees that serve them. No matter how great the product or service or organizational structure is, without happy employees or customers, most businesses will not last.

Greed never wins.

As a leader, what are your business and personal measures of success? Are they aligned? What's more important, hitting your quarterly projection or building a solid business that lasts? Or creating a team who rallies around a clear and convicting vision, mission, and purpose to best serve all who interact with the company and its products and services? The bigger question is, how can you accomplish both and still smile at yourself when you look in the mirror?

Into Action/Practice/Get Busy With It:

Write down ten things you have done in the past five years that you are proud of. Look at that list. How do you feel when you revisit those moments? As you accomplished them, would you say you felt successful? Also take note of who you have helped and how you have improved the lives of others or the communities and organizations you serve.

Now, as you move forward, find more opportunities to do things like those and start stacking them up like wood for your winter cabin. As you do, you may even rekindle the fire that's been slowly turning into ash. Keep it stoked and you will be successful wherever you go and whatever you do.

Remember you are in control. Success is whatever you decide it to be.

Room to Write, Reflect & Respond

Consider these questions/prompts when and where they're appropriate:

What does this prompt stir in you?

Positive	Negative

What resistance, if any do you feel and where?

For example: Before I speak or make cold-calls I feel a knot in my throat and tightness in my belly.

Old Story	New Story

What if... Consider the worst-case scenario and ask yourself if it's likely to happen or just fear. Then reframe each problem/challenge into an opportunity.

Evaluate the Risks & Rewards of Action/Inaction

Risk	Reward

Action	Inaction

If what you want is necessary and important, decide to act right now.

If not, let it go. Unless or until it becomes important, it's not and is an energy drain.

Ask and Commit

What **one thing** can you do to change/let go of/advance that will make you happier and bring you peace and joy?

Thoughts:

Feelings:

Potential Actions:

Finally, write a Positive Affirmation/Mantra that will help support and manifest your ideal new story.

The Power of Belief

See it. Say it. Believe it. Do it. This is a simple mantra of manifestation I have used throughout my life that can be incredibly powerful if you believe in it and yourself.

Today we're going to do a little belief practice.

Into Action/Practice/Get Busy With It:
Grab a piece of paper and draw a line down the middle. At the top of the left column, put a plus sign. At the top of the right column, a minus sign.

Starting with the right column, list every single negative thing about yourself that you do not like or that you would like to change. Don't wallow or assess, just write. Take five minutes to do this now.

Now read what you have written. How do these things make you feel? Which are really troublesome? Which do you think are easy to change? Which have you struggled with for a while and are sick and tired of letting them get to you? Which have caused the most pain, fear, anxiety? Which have interfered with some aspect of your life? For example, what consequences have carrying these negative emotions had in your personal relationships, with your work, or with your self-esteem and self-confidence? **Circle those.**

Next, repeat the process for the plus column. Write down every single thing you like about yourself. What you are good at? What brings you joy or makes you happy? Which make you feel lighter and not heavy or burdened? Which would you like to do or experience more often? Which have helped you feel more alive, productive, or given you a positive outlook on the direction of your life? **Circle those.**

Now, review those you circled on the right (-) and those on the left (+). What does the pattern tell you? Are there more on one side vs. the other?

What do you see on the right? What emotions do you feel? For example, when you look at those circled on the right do you feel sadness? Anger? Disappointment?

Do the same for the left. What do you see? How do they make you feel? Which do you want more of? For most, the answer is likely those on the left.

Now ask yourself these very important questions: What needs to change about those on the right so I can feel better about myself? Which side do I want to add to? Which are true? Which make me feel better about myself? Which would I rather think about? Which am I willing to change? What will help me find the courage to do something different?

When you are done, **let go of your attachment to any outcome**.

This is the secret of manifesting change and building belief.

The secret you've been seeking isn't found in theories or shiny new strategies. It's hidden under our noses in plain sight; in willingness and action, without certainty of the outcome.

To trust in that which you cannot see, taste, touch, feel…yet. For this exercise to be effective, you must surrender and be 100% willing to get into some form of action to manifest that which you seek. In other words, *no practice, no progress*.

Seek. Ask. Find. Do.

As you do, your belief will grow even stronger, creating unshakeable confidence because you are an active participant in creating the life you want, not an unconfident bystander watching life pass you by.

Room to Write, Reflect & Respond

Consider these questions/prompts when and where they're appropriate:

What does this prompt stir in you?

Positive	Negative

What resistance, if any do you feel and where?

For example: Before I speak or make cold-calls I feel a knot in my throat and tightness in my belly.

Old Story	New Story

What if... Consider the worst-case scenario and ask yourself if it's likely to happen or just fear. Then reframe each problem/challenge into an opportunity.

Evaluate the Risks & Rewards of Action/Inaction

Risk	Reward

Action	Inaction

If what you want is necessary and important, decide to act right now.

If not, let it go. Unless or until it becomes important, it's not and is an energy drain.

Ask and Commit

What **one thing** can you do to change/let go of/advance that will make you happier and bring you peace and joy?

Thoughts:

Feelings:

Potential Actions:

Finally, write a Positive Affirmation/Mantra that will help support and manifest your ideal new story.

Practice Daily Acts of Kindness

We've all heard and perhaps participated in or been the recipient of random acts of kindness. From simple things such as holding the door open for a young mother with an infant in her arms, to paying it forward or passing on some gift as at the drive-thru of your favorite coffee shop.

Today I encourage you to look for more opportunities to spread unconditional goodwill. There are numerous service organizations, clubs, or associations which offer opportunities to serve, volunteer or belong. Consider finding one that may fulfill a purpose greater than your own needs.

Why?

Because anytime we take our eyes off ourselves and focus on serving the needs of others, we tend to feel better about ourselves. As the saying goes, it's truly better to give than receive.

Research suggests that we spend over **95% of our waking time thinking about ourselves. According to the National Science Foundation, 80% of our thoughts are negative and 95% of our thoughts are repetitive. It's no wonder why, according to other studies, 85% of us suffer from low self-esteem.** How sad. It may be tempting to want to dig in and ask why. We can even consult with mental health professionals, doctors, therapists, and psychologists to get at the root causes and conditions of why. And there is nothing wrong with that. But let's start with something more practical that any of us can do—be a little kinder to ourselves.

What are some ways we can treat ourselves kindly? We can disrupt the deeply entrenched patterns of negative self-talk, and bat away fear, worry, and self-doubt. We can stop perpetuating negative thoughts about ourselves and the world around us. We can face our limitations instead of defending them. We can stop protecting our feelings through justification, denial, or some other coping mechanism.

Try this instead: *practice saying, being, and treating ourselves with the love and respect we would want others to treat us with.*

More specifically, **you may want to practice some form of self-care.** Get a mani-pedi, a massage, treat yourself to a meal, go on a date, do something that makes you smile and feel happy. Perhaps that is offering to serve the homeless at the local soup kitchen or volunteer at your kid's school. Whatever it is, be intentional about your awareness when the negativity creeps in. Make a conscious decision to not feed it or run with it. Find something that makes you smile to replace those negative thoughts.

In short, **do more of the things that bring you joy, and stop wasting your precious time and energy worrying about things that are not helpful and probably will never happen.**

Room to Write, Reflect & Respond

Consider these questions/prompts when and where they're appropriate:

What does this prompt stir in you?

Positive	Negative

What resistance, if any do you feel and where?

For example: Before I speak or make cold-calls I feel a knot in my throat and tightness in my belly.

Old Story	New Story

What if... Consider the worst-case scenario and ask yourself if it's likely to happen or just fear. Then reframe each problem/challenge into an opportunity.

Evaluate the Risks & Rewards of Action/Inaction

Risk	Reward

Action	Inaction

If what you want is necessary and important, decide to act right now.

If not, let it go. Unless or until it becomes important, it's not and is an energy drain.

Ask and Commit

What **one thing** can you do to change/let go of/advance that will make you happier and bring you peace and joy?

Thoughts:

Feelings:

Potential Actions:

Finally, write a Positive Affirmation/Mantra that will help support and manifest your ideal new story.

The Secret Power of Prayer, Meditation, and Visualization

For me, prayer, meditation, and creative visualization help connect my abilities and imagination to a giant conduit of possibility, the sum of all thought and creative energy.

So, the question becomes, how can we tap into this invisible power to benefit ourselves and others at will? I can't answer that for you. That is a matter of personal desire, motivation, need, and belief. It's one of the great mysteries of this thing we call life.

But I don't want to leave you hanging like that.

What is Prayer?

In simple terms, prayer is an act of introspection and inquiry; a conversation with ourselves, God, or what you consider spiritual. Prayer can be whatever it means to you. Prayer for me is all about *asking*. Meditation is all about *listening*.

Prayer is also asking and waiting for guidance from a source that is not our own minds. This source can be whatever you chose to call it: Higher Power, The Universe, Mother Nature, God, Allah, Buddha, Yahweh, etc. To me, the name is not nearly as important as the act of praying.

I pray a lot and when I do, my days go smoother. Not always, but frequently enough that it's become a healthy habit. Why? Because I like smooth days.

What is Meditation?

In essence, *meditation is about being present long enough to still our minds and allow thoughts to unfold without judgment.* It's about awareness and presence, feeling and listening to what our minds and bodies are trying to tell us, and not trying to fix anything in our meditative moments.

What is Creative Visualization?

Creative visualization is comprised of one or more mindfulness exercises for the purpose of manifesting and promoting success in every area of life.

Visualization can be creating vision or dream boards, or daydreaming about a desired shift, change, or outcome one would like to manifest in their life. It may include some form of prayer and meditation. Of seeing the end in mind before taking action. Calling upon and trusting in the powers of the creative universe, to clearly see and believe what we can be, have, or do, then find the courage and faith to work toward fulfilling that vison.

These three disciplines, principles, or habits of prayer, meditation, and creative visualization are critical components which will help us reframe and reprogram *how* and *what* we *think* and *believe* about ourselves and others. They are *holistic, encompassing, connecting*.

What areas of your life can you begin to practice one or more of these? How might they help you find clarity, courage, and conviction? If any resistance comes up as you think of each ask deeper questions, for example, *what is the resistance trying to teach me?*

The answers you seek will come as you listen to what the resistance has to say. When it shows up as an unannounced solicitor in your mind you have a choice—find the courage to try something new or different, or let it continue to control you.

Whatever you choose, remain steadfast and clear about your motives and intentions, then take action to manifest your destiny.

Room to Write, Reflect & Respond

Consider these questions/prompts when and where they're appropriate:

What does this prompt stir in you?

Positive	Negative

What resistance, if any do you feel and where?

For example: Before I speak or make cold-calls I feel a knot in my throat and tightness in my belly.

Old Story	New Story

What if... Consider the worst-case scenario and ask yourself if it's likely to happen or just fear. Then reframe each problem/challenge into an opportunity.

Evaluate the Risks & Rewards of Action/Inaction

Risk	Reward

Action	Inaction

If what you want is necessary and important, decide to act right now.

If not, let it go. Unless or until it becomes important, it's not and is an energy drain.

Ask and Commit

What **one thing** can you do to change/let go of/advance that will make you happier and bring you peace and joy?

Thoughts:

Feelings:

Potential Actions:

Finally, write a Positive Affirmation/Mantra that will help support and manifest your ideal new story.

Action, Not Words

The road to freedom of any type is not paved with good intentions, nor is it a straight and narrow path.

Any worthy transformation or liberation starts with recognition of something that must change and is usually driven by avoidance of pain or desire for pleasure. Something we must desperately escape from like a bad relationship, job, or addiction. Or something we absolutely must have like freedom, independence, meaning, purpose, and success.

How often do we think about all the things we would like to be, do, or have, and how great our lives would be if we had them?

One day, we may be all excited about the next best thing we're gonna do and how it will make us fitter, faster, better looking, richer or empower us to become another demigod determined to change the world. We may even go on and on spinning visions of grandeur and grandiose dreams in our own heads or with our closest friends or anyone willing to listen. But are thinking and talking ever a direct path into action? Usually, the answer is no.

What happens to most of us? That's right, we stay in the talking and thinking stage and may even take a few steps toward what we want, such as joining a gym or signing up for the next "masterclass." We may feel empowered for a day, or a week, maybe even a month. But then our inner critics speak up. When they do, what happens? Suddenly we give up faster than we got started. Or worse, we just keep talking, never taking any further meaningful action.

Why? Fear of more rejection? Failure? Or success?

I don't know. But I do know that we all suffer from imposter syndrome, self-doubt, and a tendency to overthink things, and it is killing our hopes and dreams of what may be great ideas.

What's the solution? **Bold action. Guts. Courage.** A willingness to take a chance on ourselves and more importantly a **willingness to fall down and fail, then getting back up again until we succeed.**

Simply put, it means *action, not words.* And success is found in consistent practice and discipline over time. Incremental improvement. Habit stacking. Confidence building. And finding some form of a support/accountability group to help pick you up when you feel like giving up.

None of this is new. Yet why do so many still grapple with feeling better on the inside while trying their hardest to look good on the outside? I do not know. But the struggle is real on some level for all of us, regardless of who we are or where we are in life.

Perhaps knowing that we are not alone will make it easier for us to stop trying so hard to have immediate results and instead accept that if we really want something different, it will take guts, willingness, and *consistent* effort over time to ever change.

Into Action/Practice/Get Busy With It:
What areas of your own life need a bold move or lifestyle change? What's preventing you from doing it now? Make a list and start finding ways to take immediate, intentional, and frequent action, then get busy with it.

Room to Write, Reflect & Respond

Consider these questions/prompts when and where they're appropriate:

What does this prompt stir in you?

Positive	Negative

What resistance, if any do you feel and where?

For example: Before I speak or make cold-calls I feel a knot in my throat and tightness in my belly.

Old Story	New Story

What if… Consider the worst-case scenario and ask yourself if it's likely to happen or just fear. Then reframe each problem/challenge into an opportunity.

Evaluate the Risks & Rewards of Action/Inaction

Risk	Reward

Action	Inaction

If what you want is necessary and important, decide to act right now.

If not, let it go. Unless or until it becomes important, it's not and is an energy drain.

Ask and Commit

What **one thing** can you do to change/let go of/advance that will make you happier and bring you peace and joy?

Thoughts:

Feelings:

Potential Actions:

Finally, write a Positive Affirmation/Mantra that will help support and manifest your ideal new story.

Do Your Best, Always

Progress, not perfection. I first heard this phrase in early recovery over three decades ago. It has been a mantra ever since. Anytime I face challenges or venture into the deep end of the pool without my floaties, I must remember I am no longer a toddler and know how to swim.

It took a lot of patience by my dad to teach me how to swim. Just as it did when he taught me how to ride a bike. I fell down a lot. One day I almost ran into a busy street because I didn't yet know how to use the brakes. Fortunately, my dad was fast enough to catch me before I got hit by a bus.

What are some areas that you tend to overthink because you expect to be perfect? Work? Life? Money? Relationships? What creative ideas have you been thinking about but haven't started because you want to get all the facts and figures—your ducks—in a row first?

I have a challenge for you—how would you like to feel more alive than you may have in the past year? Think back to when you learned to ride a bike or swim (assuming you can), how did it feel when you finally "got it"?

Into Action/Practice/Get Busy With It:
Now take a few minutes to consider one area of your life or a project that has been nagging you because you want it to be perfect. Perhaps you have been stuck in analysis paralysis and haven't even started it, whatever it is. Honestly consider, what's blocking you? Is it some kind of fear? A belief tied to your perceived worth or value? Of yourself or to others? What is *it*? How do you feel now? *How would you like to feel?*

Now pretend you have a magic pair of glasses. They give you the superpower of boldness. Put them on and look at your project/area of self-improvement you want and trust that whatever you do to start or take the next step forward is going to make you feel 10x better than if you keep waiting for everything to be perfect.

Now that you have no more excuses and bling superpower sunglasses, it's to get busy.

Start by **doing one thing** to move you closer to whatever it is you want to manifest in your life.

As you do, it's wise to take time to celebrate your wins, large or small, in ways that bring you joy. The rest is simple: keep doing the next best thing, because in the end, that's more than enough to get you from where you are to where you want to be.

Plus, **your best is all you can ever do anyway.** So, why not lighten up and get jiggy with it?

Room to Write, Reflect & Respond

Consider these questions/prompts when and where they're appropriate:

What does this prompt stir in you?

Positive	Negative

What resistance, if any do you feel and where?

For example: Before I speak or make cold-calls I feel a knot in my throat and tightness in my belly.

Old Story	New Story

What if... Consider the worst-case scenario and ask yourself if it's likely to happen or just fear. Then reframe each problem/challenge into an opportunity.

Evaluate the Risks & Rewards of Action/Inaction

Risk	Reward

Action	Inaction

If what you want is necessary and important, decide to act right now.

If not, let it go. Unless or until it becomes important, it's not and is an energy drain.

Ask and Commit

What **one thing** can you do to change/let go of/advance that will make you happier and bring you peace and joy?

Thoughts:

Feelings:

Potential Actions:

Finally, write a Positive Affirmation/Mantra that will help support and manifest your ideal new story.

I Will...Until

Determination. Courage. Incrementalism. Practice. Habit Stacking. Confidence building. Belief. Knowing. Each of these are integral components for developing a growth-oriented mindset. One that promotes success, accomplishment, achievement, inner peace, or whatever it is that you want to manifest into a new state of being or purpose.

With accomplishment, there is no final destination. No end. Only perpetual new beginnings.

Success is a process marked by victories, milestones, and landmarks along your journey. Essentially, "I will ...Until" is a success-oriented mindset that is **focused, driven, and dynamic.**

In this sense, I would define success as *a unique and individual commitment to persistent and intentional personal growth and improvement for maximum benefit to all.*

In other words, as you do you become. As you advance, there you are. As you give, you receive. The above definition includes three pillars to creating an extraordinary life:

1. *A unique and individual commitment*
2. *to persistent and intentional personal growth and improvement*
3. *for maximum benefit to all*

Any worthy endeavor must be driven by determination and courage to do whatever it takes to succeed. It is and always will be an inside job driven by you and whatever energy you believe empowers you and your life.

Through incremental shifts and continuous improvements over time, we develop newer and better habits. Eventually, they become solid gold confidence bricks for us to safely store in our confidence bank for those days when we may need a little encouragement.

As we continue to practice and fail, we begin to adapt and develop a keen sense of what works and what does not. With each new skill, habit, or victory, we ultimately get to a place where we not only believe we can be, do, or have that which we seek, *we know we will succeed*. We *know* because we are committed to the long game firmly believing that *we will, until.*

Bonus Prompt:
Repeat the following Manifestation and Motivational Mantra:

My success is inevitable! Shout it out until you feel it somewhere in your body.

Repeat it often whenever you begin to doubt. And if you really want to believe it and make it happen, make sure to **shout it out loud!**

Room to Write, Reflect & Respond

Consider these questions/prompts when and where they're appropriate:

What does this prompt stir in you?

Positive	Negative

What resistance, if any do you feel and where?

For example: Before I speak or make cold-calls I feel a knot in my throat and tightness in my belly.

Old Story	New Story

What if... Consider the worst-case scenario and ask yourself if it's likely to happen or just fear. Then reframe each problem/challenge into an opportunity.

Evaluate the Risks & Rewards of Action/Inaction

Risk	Reward

Action	Inaction

If what you want is necessary and important, decide to act right now.
If not, let it go. Unless or until it becomes important, it's not and is an energy drain.

Ask and Commit
What **one thing** can you do to change/let go of/advance that will make you happier and bring you peace and joy?

Thoughts:

Feelings:

Potential Actions:

Finally, write a Positive Affirmation/Mantra that will help support and manifest your ideal new story.

Acceptance and Detachment

Bad things happen to good people. Good things happen to bad people. All the time. Who cares?

Our happiness or success is not determined by the perception of or comparison to others. Success is not always a race. It is whatever you decide it to be. Your reasons. Your KPI's (key performance indicators). You make the rules. Sure, you may have expectations for your job that you must meet, but even those can be modified to align with your own measures of success.

Here's a simple commitment statement that can be used by anyone whether for personal or business goals: **I do the best I can and leave the results up to the universe.**

I can hear some of you now saying, *Wait, that's bullshit, you don't know the pressure I am under. You don't have my boss. You don't know how demanding my customers are. What about the shareholders and leaders?*

Yeah, what about them? If they hired you or you hired them, did you fully vet them and make an informed decision that they were the most qualified candidates for the role and position at the time you hired or acquired them?

Then why not trust them to do their best and let go of all the things that are completely out of their or your control? And if their plans for _____ (fill in the blank) didn't result in the specific outcome sought, accept the results, learn from them, and keep adjusting the plan until all parties are happy with the results. Or, of course, replace them and make sure you make a better hiring decision next time.

What I mean is we must give agency to the process of trial and error, both individually and collectively. We must not only **allow and accept failure.** To thrive and grow we must encourage it.

There can be no success without a failure first.

Why?

Because lasting and meaningful success in any endeavor or business requires 100% acceptance that *failure is integral to any solution.* Equally important, we must also detach completely from the expectations of results at every phase and trial. As we practice this mental shift, we will free our creative energy to be more solution focused rather than stuck in a perpetual detrimental state ruled by fear of failure.

In short, here's the paradox: **as we embrace our failures and accept them and learn to let go of our expectations, we will ultimately succeed wherever we go and at whatever we do.**

Into Action/Practice/Get Busy With It:
For your consideration…

What areas of your life are you challenged with trying to accept? What improvements can be made? What are your expectations?

If also a leader, are your expectations clearly communicated to others? If not, why? What is the impact on your company's bottom line for lack of clarity, communication, vision, mission, or purpose? How can you fix that? How happy are the members of your team? How happy are you?

Room to Write, Reflect & Respond

Consider these questions/prompts when and where they're appropriate:

What does this prompt stir in you?

Positive	Negative

What resistance, if any do you feel and where?

For example: Before I speak or make cold-calls I feel a knot in my throat and tightness in my belly.

Old Story	New Story

What if... Consider the worst-case scenario and ask yourself if it's likely to happen or just fear. Then reframe each problem/challenge into an opportunity.

Evaluate the Risks & Rewards of Action/Inaction

Risk	Reward

Action	Inaction

If what you want is necessary and important, decide to act right now.

If not, let it go. Unless or until it becomes important, it's not and is an energy drain.

Ask and Commit

What **one thing** can you do to change/let go of/advance that will make you happier and bring you peace and joy?

Thoughts:

Feelings:

Potential Actions:

Finally, write a Positive Affirmation/Mantra that will help support and manifest your ideal new story.

Focus on What You Can Control and Let Go of What You Can't

I have found my days to be much smoother when I stop trying to control people, places and things where I have none. When I remain in a state of acceptance and surrender, I am less stressed. This has not come easily. I have had many missteps and continue to catch myself when I am trying to take control of situations. This is likely a foreign concept for many who have spent their entire lives trying to create the world they want. The key lies in knowing what you can control, such as your thoughts, actions, and beliefs, and how you can focus your energy in a manner that improves your life or the lives of those around you. It is about using the full breadth of your mental, physical, emotional, and spiritual gifts so they align with a greater purpose or worldview.

Likewise, the emotionally and socially mature person will refrain from vain attempts to control things they cannot. The balance between control and surrender is where we find serenity and inner peace.

Into Action/Practice/Get Busy With It:
Awareness Exercise:

Take a few minutes to look at one or more areas of your life where you may be feeling the resistance to something and become aware of how you typically respond when things do not go according to your plans. Recognize what is within your control and how best to approach a challenging circumstance, personal or otherwise. Sit with it and don't fight it. If an answer comes to you that is within your control, do that. If it's not in your control, let it go.

Remain mindful of your decisions for the next few days and apply this simple process of awareness and waiting before reacting or responding. See if you feel better and more in control. If you do, keep at it. Eventually this new practice will become a normal part of your decision-making process and ultimately a habit worth mastering and teaching to others.

Room to Write, Reflect & Respond

Consider these questions/prompts when and where they're appropriate:

What does this prompt stir in you?

Positive	Negative

What resistance, if any do you feel and where?

For example: Before I speak or make cold-calls I feel a knot in my throat and tightness in my belly.

Old Story	New Story

What if... Consider the worst-case scenario and ask yourself if it's likely to happen or just fear. Then reframe each problem/challenge into an opportunity.

Evaluate the Risks & Rewards of Action/Inaction

Risk	Reward

Action	Inaction

If what you want is necessary and important, decide to act right now.

If not, let it go. Unless or until it becomes important, it's not and is an energy drain.

Ask and Commit

What **one thing** can you do to change/let go of/advance that will make you happier and bring you peace and joy?

Thoughts:

Feelings:

Potential Actions:

Finally, write a Positive Affirmation/Mantra that will help support and manifest your ideal new story.

Room to Write, Reflect & Respond

Consider these questions/prompts when and where they're appropriate:

What does this prompt stir in you?

Positive	Negative

What resistance, if any do you feel and where?

For example: Before I speak or make cold-calls I feel a knot in my throat and tightness in my belly.

Old Story	New Story

What if... Consider the worst-case scenario and ask yourself if it's likely to happen or just fear. Then reframe each problem/challenge into an opportunity.

Evaluate the Risks & Rewards of Action/Inaction

Risk	Reward

Action	Inaction

If what you want is necessary and important, decide to act right now.
If not, let it go. Unless or until it becomes important, it's not and is an energy drain.

Ask and Commit
What **one thing** can you do to change/let go of/advance that will make you happier and bring you peace and joy?

Thoughts:

Feelings:

Potential Actions:

Finally, write a Positive Affirmation/Mantra that will help support and manifest your ideal new story.

Massive Action

I've been in sales for more than three decades. It's common practice for sales reps to have a goal or quota to hit in exchange for a reward in the form of commission. But inevitably there are times where I have faced a gap between my actual sales and what the company expectations are. When that happens, I have choices—throw in the towel and hope the next month is better. Quit. Or dramatically increase my level of meaningful activity and purposeful effort—massive action.

Over the years I have done all three, but the greatest rewards have been found when I redoubled or even tripled my efforts to hit goal. That usually consists of increased effort in these three key areas: prospecting, research, and invitation by email or cold call.

By repeating behaviors that produce results, I build confidence and belief. Fear no longer runs my life. The same is true for anything we want to learn or eventually master; **we need to practice a lot.** We need to get our reps in. **We need massive action to break bad habits and build better ones.**

The velocity and pace of our massive action will vary depending in the urgency we have. We must know our why and keep it top of mind. Some of us may need to come from a place of desperation, as with mental, physical, or emotional crises. For our survival we may need to take prudent and aggressive measures in an attempt to heal.

But one thing is certain, if we are to create, we must act. And if we want something bad enough, or the urgency is greater than our fear, we must not only be bold enough to start but consistent in our level of activity if we are to find resolution.

For your consideration…

When have you wanted something so bad that you were all in? What happened? What did you do to get it?

Room to Write, Reflect & Respond
Consider these questions/prompts when and where they're appropriate:

What does this prompt stir in you?

Positive	Negative

What resistance, if any do you feel and where?
For example: Before I speak or make cold-calls I feel a knot in my throat and tightness in my belly.

Old Story	New Story

What if… Consider the worst-case scenario and ask yourself if it's likely to happen or just fear. Then reframe each problem/challenge into an opportunity.

Evaluate the Risks & Rewards of Action/Inaction

Risk	Reward

Action	Inaction

If what you want is necessary and important, decide to act right now.

If not, let it go. Unless or until it becomes important, it's not and is an energy drain.

Ask and Commit

What **one thing** can you do to change/let go of/advance that will make you happier and bring you peace and joy?

Thoughts:

Feelings:

Potential Actions:

Finally, write a Positive Affirmation/Mantra that will help support and manifest your ideal new story.

Confidence is a Product, Not a Prerequisite of Success

There's a common misperception many ambitious people make—they wait for confidence to come before they get started.

That's not how it works.

Confidence is a product of discipline, motivation, and effort. It also requires willingness, courage and belief. Put simply, we become confident when we muster the courage to take a chance on ourselves and boldly step into unchartered territory, the unknown, and begin the process of trial and error toward a worthy aim. With each failure or success, we build knowledge and gain valuable experience which increases our self-confidence.

Discipline, motivation, and effort are the pillars of building confidence. Without effort, we will never know what it means to be confident. And *when we know*, because we have done, that is *confidence*. Until we risk our ego or pride and take a chance on ourselves, we will never become fully confident in our skills or abilities.

Confidence is a product of *doing* and *being*.

The doing part is easy. It's the being part that often trips us up because we look at becoming confident as a destination or an arrival. The same approach many of us use for our goals.

Those strategies, without a clear motive or reason why seldom work.

They don't work because we are too busy looking for short-cuts.

There are none.

Confidence is a state of being that arises by doing and failing. It is also an attitude, like happiness. If we want to be happy, we choose to be happy.

I know I am oversimplifying it, but that is precisely my point—**don't overthink it.**

If you want to became more confident, decide to do what it takes and **be more confident.**

There are many ways to building "unshakeable" self-confidence. The ones that stick and have the greatest long-term impact are those earned by and through frequent failure.

So, the key to being more self-confident isn't found by failing less. If you want to win, you must fail more. Lots more, and hopefully learn a few things about you and your process as you do. This is not only the key to building confidence, it, in many respects, is yet one more pearl of ancient wisdom to success and happiness.

The faster you find the courage to fail more often, the better. But, if you decide to stay stuck dawdling in the caves of fear, doubt, and indecision, and don't do what it takes to earn it—well then, you know.

Room to Write, Reflect & Respond

Consider these questions/prompts when and where they're appropriate:

What does this prompt stir in you?

Positive	Negative

What resistance, if any do you feel and where?

For example: Before I speak or make cold-calls I feel a knot in my throat and tightness in my belly.

Old Story	New Story

What if... Consider the worst-case scenario and ask yourself if it's likely to happen or just fear. Then reframe each problem/challenge into an opportunity.

Evaluate the Risks & Rewards of Action/Inaction

Risk	Reward

Action	Inaction

If what you want is necessary and important, decide to act right now.

If not, let it go. Unless or until it becomes important, it's not and is an energy drain.

Ask and Commit

What **one thing** can you do to change/let go of/advance that will make you happier and bring you peace and joy?

Thoughts:

Feelings:

Potential Actions:

Finally, write a Positive Affirmation/Mantra that will help support and manifest your ideal new story.

Crossing Bridges over Rivers of Fear and Unmet Dreams

I love the Jimmy Cliff song, "Many Rivers to Cross." We will cross many rivers in our lifetime: rivers of fear, doubt, uncertainty, and loss, as well as rivers of dreams, hopes, and love.

The rivers will always be there, often with a bridge offering safe passage to the other side. We need only look for it and stop staring at the river's muddy edge littered with rusty bicycles, water bottles, and discarded tires.

Our task and responsibility is simple: **to become keenly aware of the bridges and life rafts the universe places before us and to be bold or desperate enough to use them.**

Room to Write, Reflect & Respond

Consider these questions/prompts when and where they're appropriate:

What does this prompt stir in you?

Positive	Negative

What resistance, if any do you feel and where?

For example: Before I speak or make cold-calls I feel a knot in my throat and tightness in my belly.

Old Story	New Story

What if... Consider the worst-case scenario and ask yourself if it's likely to happen or just fear. Then reframe each problem/challenge into an opportunity.

Evaluate the Risks & Rewards of Action/Inaction

Risk	Reward

Action	Inaction

If what you want is necessary and important, decide to act right now.
If not, let it go. Unless or until it becomes important, it's not and is an energy drain.

Ask and Commit
What **one thing** can you do to change/let go of/advance that will make you happier and bring you peace and joy?

Thoughts:

Feelings:

Potential Actions:

Finally, write a Positive Affirmation/Mantra that will help support and manifest your ideal new story.

The Path is the Path

Choices. Decisions. Questioning. Second-guessing. Are we on the right path? To what? Is there a better path? If so, where is it? How do we find it? How will we know if we are on the "right path"? What if we are going the wrong way? Then what?

Does anyone else ever have looping thoughts like these? What happens when you do? Do your palms sweat? Does your heart rate increase? Does panic set in? Or are you so confident that you are on the right path that you refuse to ask or take directions, or even admit that you may be going the wrong way?

What will it mean if you travel along the path for a bit and realize that you may want to turn off the trail toward a majestic waterfall you see in the distance? Does that make you wrong for not choosing that path to begin with?

No.

The path you chose is the path you are on. And you can always choose a different one. The path will not hold a grudge if you do. Which will you choose? And will you be OK with what you decide?

The catch-22 is that sometimes you can only make an informed decision to take a different path once you traverse further along the one you are on. The best part is *you hold the power and freedom to choose your own path. What will you do?*

Room to Write, Reflect & Respond
Consider these questions/prompts when and where they're appropriate:

What does this prompt stir in you?

Positive	Negative

What resistance, if any do you feel and where?
For example: Before I speak or make cold-calls I feel a knot in my throat and tightness in my belly.

Old Story	New Story

What if... Consider the worst-case scenario and ask yourself if it's likely to happen or just fear. Then reframe each problem/challenge into an opportunity.

Evaluate the Risks & Rewards of Action/Inaction

Risk	Reward

Action	Inaction

If what you want is necessary and important, decide to act right now.

If not, let it go. Unless or until it becomes important, it's not and is an energy drain.

Ask and Commit

What **one thing** can you do to change/let go of/advance that will make you happier and bring you peace and joy?

Thoughts:

Feelings:

Potential Actions:

Finally, write a Positive Affirmation/Mantra that will help support and manifest your ideal new story.

Letting Go of Expectations

Several years ago, a podcast host recommend reading *Expectation Hangover* by Christine Hassler. I immediately bought it and read it in three days. It totally hit home. I related to so much of what she said about our need to detach and let go of our expectations about many things, especially our mindset about self-worth and value as well as what we expect others to do. If you struggle with co-dependency, imposter syndrome, or control issues, I highly recommend it.

On a personal level, I still struggle with expectations all the time. On the one hand it seems normal to expect certain things as a result of our effort. On the other hand, we may set ourselves up for disappointment when we place expectations on things we cannot control.

In recovery I heard the phrase, "our level of serenity is inversely proportional to our level of expectation." It bugged me then and it still bugs me now.

Why?

Because as mentioned earlier, most of us get upset when things don't go our way.

I recall an incident in my first year of recovery that cost me my job as a result of unmet expectations. One of my first jobs was slinging enchiladas and margaritas at a busy Mexican restaurant. I hated it. The tips were lousy and I thought I deserved to work in a classier restaurant.

One busy night I had a four-top (four customers) sit in my section. It started out fine until the customers kept ordering more margaritas, one at a time every time I came back to the table. I was happy they were spending more money but was irritated because I was busy and they weren't ordering the way I expected them to.

Each time I asked if anyone else would like one or if they would like to get a pitcher instead. The answer was always the same, "No. Just mine."

Long story short, this continued and by the end of the night I was fuming inside but trying not let it show. When they paid the bill, they said to "keep the change." The change was a meager $5 tip.
As politely as I could. I asked if there was anything wrong with the service they said, "Yeah, we don't like your attitude."

I lost it and told them to get the hell out of my restaurant. Not a good move. I was fired on the spot.

I let these customers get under my skin because I expected a 20% tip. I lost my serenity because my expectations were not met. In truth, I wanted a different job because I didn't like serving so much alcohol and thought I deserved to work in a classier restaurant.

Into Action/Practice/Get Busy With It:
Re-read this, "our level of serenity is inversely proportional to our level of expectation."

What, if anything comes up for you? Are there some areas of disappointment you are facing? How do you feel? Did you have expectations of something working out the way *you* wanted and it didn't? What are these feelings saying to you? How might you approach a similar situation differently, next time?

Room to Write, Reflect & Respond

Consider these questions/prompts when and where they're appropriate:

What does this prompt stir in you?

Positive	Negative

What resistance, if any do you feel and where?

For example: Before I speak or make cold-calls I feel a knot in my throat and tightness in my belly.

Old Story	New Story

What if… Consider the worst-case scenario and ask yourself if it's likely to happen or just fear. Then reframe each problem/challenge into an opportunity.

Evaluate the Risks & Rewards of Action/Inaction

Risk	Reward

Action	Inaction

If what you want is necessary and important, decide to act right now.

If not, let it go. Unless or until it becomes important, it's not and is an energy drain.

Ask and Commit

What **one thing** can you do to change/let go of/advance that will make you happier and bring you peace and joy?

Thoughts:

Feelings:

Potential Actions:

Finally, write a Positive Affirmation/Mantra that will help support and manifest your ideal new story.

Love and Acceptance

Love is one of the most often used words and themes in music, movies, and books. It's richly loaded with a full breadth and depth of our emotional experience as humans, as connected beings in this journey we call life. Love has the power to save lives and if abused, can also destroy them.

Closely tied to love is another less popular but equally powerful word, acceptance. *Acceptance is love manifested.* Love of ourselves. Love by accepting others as they are no matter how different they may be from us; no matter the degree of pain and suffering they may be facing compared to our own or lack thereof.

Love is accepting people, places, and things as they are. Unconditionally, without any expectations. To expect something in exchange for love is not love. It is manipulation.

True love is what it is. And one of the most powerful manifestations of love can be seen in a mother's love for their child. As with mine, who loved and accepted me enough as I was, in my addiction, until I made the decision to find help and become sober. She loved me until I learned to love myself. And so, it is and always will be.

Whether reciprocated or not, love begets love.

Challenge:
What areas can you be more loving? To yourself and others?
What will you do? How will it make you feel?
Are you willing to love a little bit more every day? If so, how?

Room to Write, Reflect & Respond

Consider these questions/prompts when and where they're appropriate:

What does this prompt stir in you?

Positive	Negative

What resistance, if any do you feel and where?

For example: Before I speak or make cold-calls I feel a knot in my throat and tightness in my belly.

Old Story	New Story

What if... Consider the worst-case scenario and ask yourself if it's likely to happen or just fear. Then reframe each problem/challenge into an opportunity.

Evaluate the Risks & Rewards of Action/Inaction

Risk	Reward

Action	Inaction

If what you want is necessary and important, decide to act right now.

If not, let it go. Unless or until it becomes important, it's not and is an energy drain.

Ask and Commit

What **one thing** can you do to change/let go of/advance that will make you happier and bring you peace and joy?

Thoughts:

Feelings:

Potential Actions:

Finally, write a Positive Affirmation/Mantra that will help support and manifest your ideal new story.

The Disease of Loneliness: Longing to Belong

Did you know that babies can die if they are not held? Our need for physical touch does not end as infants. Like babies, we need connection and physical touch if we are to thrive. The lack of social connection poses a significant risk for individual health and longevity.

According to a 2023 report entitled, "Our Epidemic of Loneliness and Isolation: The U.S. Surgeon General's Advisory on the Healing Effects of Social Connection and Community," loneliness and social isolation increase the risk for premature death by 26% and 29% respectively. More broadly, lacking social connection can increase the risk for premature death as much as smoking up to fifteen cigarettes a day. In addition, poor or insufficient social connection is associated with increased risk of disease, including a 29% increased risk of heart disease and a 32% increased risk of stroke. Furthermore, it is associated with increased risk for anxiety, depression, and dementia. Additionally, the lack of social connection may increase susceptibility to viruses and respiratory illness.

Take away:
Want to keep loneliness at bay?
Connect with others. Show you care about yourself and others.
Reach out and hug someone, today.

Room to Write, Reflect & Respond

Consider these questions/prompts when and where they're appropriate:

What does this prompt stir in you?

Positive	Negative

What resistance, if any do you feel and where?

For example: Before I speak or make cold-calls I feel a knot in my throat and tightness in my belly.

Old Story	New Story

What if... Consider the worst-case scenario and ask yourself if it's likely to happen or just fear. Then reframe each problem/challenge into an opportunity.

Evaluate the Risks & Rewards of Action/Inaction

Risk	Reward

Action	Inaction

If what you want is necessary and important, decide to act right now.

If not, let it go. Unless or until it becomes important, it's not and is an energy drain.

Ask and Commit

What **one thing** can you do to change/let go of/advance that will make you happier and bring you peace and joy?

Thoughts:

Feelings:

Potential Actions:

Finally, write a Positive Affirmation/Mantra that will help support and manifest your ideal new story.

Creating Connection and Community

True connection is risky for many. It requires boldness and a willingness to become vulnerable enough to allow others into our own private world. To our hopes and dreams, beliefs and attitudes, and our world view. Into our mind, body, and soul. Into the secret depths of our being.

This can be scary especially if you are carrying three extra suitcases of baggage. But what if you knew you weren't the only one bringing three packed suitcases for a weekend trip to connection island? Ones stuffed with their own secrets or struggles they have dragged along for years. What if you found others who are going through whatever it is that seems so terrible that you feel all alone? As if nobody else in the world could possibly know how you feel? Do you seriously believe that you are the only one who's struggling with _____ (fill in the blank)? No. Far from it. Yet everyday there are thousands, if not millions of people who get to a place where they are sick and tired of living in the shadow of their own fears and supposed unique afflictions. Who find solace in the comfort and counsel of others. Such people make a bold decision, ask and act upon these three powerful words: **"I need help."**

Bolstered by a new level of conviction these individuals may choose to seek professionals who understand them better than they understand themselves. Or find groups of like-minded folks who have struggled or are struggling with similar or related problems. They may soon realize that *the easier, softer way through whatever is causing pain, is through connection, not isolation.*

Trust me, I know from my own struggle with addiction. There are tons of resources available for people. The only thing missing is a few seconds of courage to say, Enough! And to follow that with a decision and conviction to connect to someone else. You are worth it. Just do it.

Scores of support communities, organizations, and professionals, ready, willing, and able to assist are only a few clicks or a phone call away.

If you are struggling, *please ask for help.*

Room to Write, Reflect & Respond
Consider these questions/prompts when and where they're appropriate:

What does this prompt stir in you?

Positive	Negative

What resistance, if any do you feel and where?
For example: Before I speak or make cold-calls I feel a knot in my throat and tightness in my belly.

Old Story	New Story

What if... Consider the worst-case scenario and ask yourself if it's likely to happen or just fear. Then reframe each problem/challenge into an opportunity.

Evaluate the Risks & Rewards of Action/Inaction

Risk	Reward

Action	Inaction

If what you want is necessary and important, decide to act right now.
If not, let it go. Unless or until it becomes important, it's not and is an energy drain.

Ask and Commit

What **one thing** can you do to change/let go of/advance that will make you happier and bring you peace and joy?

Thoughts:

Feelings:

Potential Actions:

Finally, write a Positive Affirmation/Mantra that will help support and manifest your ideal new story.

Finding a Cause Worth Fighting For

Ever lose your phone, keys, sunglasses or wallet? I have several times and it can be maddening until I either find what I've lost or gone through the hassle of replacing it. What a pain!

Each of these "things" have become objective extensions and necessary tools for me to function. Though, I could I live without them, I don't want to. I suppose you wouldn't want to either and there is nothing wrong with that.

But what about other, more valuable treasures, like our family, our freedoms, or our dreams, goals, and aspirations? How important are those to us? And how do we show it? If someone met us and our family, would they know how important they are to us? If so, how? Would they feel our passion or know our calling? Do we? Is there a cause or injustice that you would like to remedy and if so, what could you do to influence a positive change?

I know this may be deep but these are important questions I consider often. Perhaps you do too.

Into Action/Practice/Get Busy With It:
Take a moment right now to pause and seriously consider some problem or circumstance bigger than you that you may be equipped to solve. Something to apply your unique set of gifts, skills, and motivation that will make your life and others or the world better because you dared to do something extraordinary. What kind of an impact do you want to have? Are you willing to invest some time, money, and energy to make a difference? What would you do? Who could you help? Why would you want to do it?

What are one or two things that you might do today to further explore this? How important would a solution be to you? To others? To the world? How bad do you want the change? Is it a cause worth fighting for?

MORNING MOTIVATION

Room to Write, Reflect & Respond

Consider these questions/prompts when and where they're appropriate:

What does this prompt stir in you?

Positive	Negative

What resistance, if any do you feel and where?

For example: Before I speak or make cold-calls I feel a knot in my throat and tightness in my belly.

Old Story	New Story

What if... Consider the worst-case scenario and ask yourself if it's likely to happen or just fear. Then reframe each problem/challenge into an opportunity.

Evaluate the Risks & Rewards of Action/Inaction

Risk	Reward

Action	Inaction

If what you want is necessary and important, decide to act right now.

If not, let it go. Unless or until it becomes important, it's not and is an energy drain.

Ask and Commit

What **one thing** can you do to change/let go of/advance that will make you happier and bring you peace and joy?

Thoughts:

Feelings:

Potential Actions:

Finally, write a Positive Affirmation/Mantra that will help support and manifest your ideal new story.

Pass it On

This simple phrase carries great weight and depth and generational significance in the context of generosity—of sharing, teaching, leading, coaching, inspiring, and much more.

Long before any of our ubiquitous advancements in communication technology, people passed on cultural wisdom through stories by campfires or etchings carved on cave or tomb walls, memorializing legacy and wisdom from generation to generation. These stories created a bond, an identity, and a sense of belonging. Wisdom of the best hunting or fishing spots, etc. were shared as a means of survival, of perpetuating a legacy for future generations.

Unfortunately, in general, our culture no longer places as high of a value on the wisdom of the elders. Instead, most of us have succumbed to incessant scroll, with oversized thumbs and glazed eyes, counting likes and sharing funny cat videos on social media. Though I have seen an increase in people sharing wisdom, spiritual awakenings, and other more meaningful milestones of their lives that may be helpful or valuable to others.

But will our social media posts have a lasting impact? Possibly, but unlikely.

How else and to whom might we share decades of earned wisdom that may leave this world a little better than when we came into it?

What legacy do you want to pass on? Why is it important? Who would you want to share it with?

Your story is valuable, especially for those who may need to hear it. When's the last time you shared a life lesson learned or a funny college anecdote with your kids? Your friends? Strangers? If you haven't, why? I encourage you to pass it on, if not for you, do it for someone else with curious ear. It may change the trajectory of someone's life or perhaps become a valuable life lesson, a legacy, one that is passed on, and on, and on…

Room to Write, Reflect & Respond

Consider these questions/prompts when and where they're appropriate:

What does this prompt stir in you?

Positive	Negative

What resistance, if any do you feel and where?

For example: Before I speak or make cold-calls I feel a knot in my throat and tightness in my belly.

Old Story	New Story

What if… Consider the worst-case scenario and ask yourself if it's likely to happen or just fear. Then reframe each problem/challenge into an opportunity.

Evaluate the Risks & Rewards of Action/Inaction

Risk	Reward

Action	Inaction

If what you want is necessary and important, decide to act right now.

If not, let it go. Unless or until it becomes important, it's not and is an energy drain.

Ask and Commit

What **one thing** can you do to change/let go of/advance that will make you happier and bring you peace and joy?

Thoughts:

Feelings:

Potential Actions:

Finally, write a Positive Affirmation/Mantra that will help support and manifest your ideal new story.

Gratitude

According to oxford languages dictionary, gratitude is: the quality of being thankful; readiness to show appreciation for and to return kindness.

"she expressed her gratitude to the committee for their support"

Gratitude is selfless, yet reciprocal.

This past Thanksgiving, I went to hug my twenty-seven-year-old son Andrew goodbye, after dinner. As he was leaving, he stopped, turned, and looked me square in the eyes and said, "Thank you for all you and mom sacrificed for me."

What does gratitude mean to you? How do you experience or express it? How does it feel to give or receive? What could you do to establish a practice of gratitude? To be more grateful?

When you have an answer, go do that. It will change your life.

Room to Write, Reflect & Respond

Consider these questions/prompts when and where they're appropriate:

What does this prompt stir in you?

Positive	Negative

What resistance, if any do you feel and where?

For example: Before I speak or make cold-calls I feel a knot in my throat and tightness in my belly.

Old Story	New Story

What if... Consider the worst-case scenario and ask yourself if it's likely to happen or just fear. Then reframe each problem/challenge into an opportunity.

Evaluate the Risks & Rewards of Action/Inaction

Risk	Reward

Action	Inaction

If what you want is necessary and important, decide to act right now.

If not, let it go. Unless or until it becomes important, it's not and is an energy drain.

Ask and Commit

What **one thing** can you do to change/let go of/advance that will make you happier and bring you peace and joy?

Thoughts:

Feelings:

Potential Actions:

Finally, write a Positive Affirmation/Mantra that will help support and manifest your ideal new story.

Victim or Victor? Taking Responsibility For How We Feel

Not all choices in life are polar opposites. Choosing to be a victim of circumstance, or a victor over whatever current battles or struggles we face is a matter of personal choice and responsibility for how we feel.

All of us vacillate between the two. Feeling like a victim, where everything is overwhelming and just too much to handle, can drive us into a pit of despair that may require professional guides to escape. I know, I've been there.

On the other end, victory may lead us to a feeling of personal pride or if we are not careful, into arrogance and cockiness. I've been there, too. Neither extremes are fun. Both are energy drains, soul sucking mindsets not conducive to creating or living happy, healthy, fulfilling lives.

What do we do? How do we break free from these polar extremes or the messy middle? Do we even want to? I can't answer that for you. That is a matter of personal choice and responsibility.

But I can assure you, from my own battles with addiction and scores of other emotional, behavioral, and relational challenges I've experienced, with few exceptions—**freedom from the bondage of self is possible.**

Into Action/Practice/Get Busy With It:
What areas of your life feel overwhelming or are causing you pain? Is it your health. Your relationships? Your confidence? Your self-esteem? What would it take to shift that? Do you even want to? What, if anything, is the pain trying to teach you? What would it feel like to be on the other side of whatever you currently feel or believe is blocking you? **Who might you ask for help?**

Room to Write, Reflect & Respond

Consider these questions/prompts when and where they're appropriate:

What does this prompt stir in you?

Positive	Negative

What resistance, if any do you feel and where?

For example: Before I speak or make cold-calls I feel a knot in my throat and tightness in my belly.

Old Story	New Story

What if... Consider the worst-case scenario and ask yourself if it's likely to happen or just fear. Then reframe each problem/challenge into an opportunity.

Evaluate the Risks & Rewards of Action/Inaction

Risk	Reward

Action	Inaction

If what you want is necessary and important, decide to act right now.
If not, let it go. Unless or until it becomes important, it's not and is an energy drain.

Ask and Commit
What **one thing** can you do to change/let go of/advance that will make you happier and bring you peace and joy?

Thoughts:

Feelings:

Potential Actions:

Finally, write a Positive Affirmation/Mantra that will help support and manifest your ideal new story.

Beware of the Itty-Bitty Shitty Committee in Your Head

Fact: Studies reveal that 85% of us suffer from low self-esteem. Other studies show, as previously mentioned, that 90% plus of our thoughts are negative. Those thoughts are what I've heard referred to as the "Itty-bitty shitty committee" in our heads.

You may be thinking, Great, way to piss me off even more, Shawn.

My pleasure. But don't get mad at me, I am just the messenger. To paraphrase a guiding principle from Al-Anon, a 12-step recovery program for co-dependency, "I didn't cause it. I can't control it. I can't fix it."

But as alluded to in the previous muse, if we want to be happier and feel better about who we are, we must take responsibility for how we feel and what we believe about ourselves. We must flip the script in our head and start telling a different story.

What does that mean?

With few exceptions, we get to choose what we say to ourselves and who we want to hang out with. If your circle of friends in your head all say the same negative shit about you, you may want to find some new friends.

Or send your inner critics to finishing school. Teach them a new language of encouragement, of hope, of confidence, of belief. Teach them some manners and stop listening to or believing what they say.

OK, but how? you may wonder.

The short answer is to ask for professional help. As previously mentioned, there are scores of resources and professionals to help guide you.

You may also consider a little honest reflection and examination of what your inner critics are saying. Some of it may actually be true because you believe them. How does what they say make you feel? Why do they keep coming back? Are you feeding them, like squirrels, seagulls, foxes, or racoons? Why? Don't they just poop all over the place after you're done tossing them peanuts or Cheetos?

Start listing out everything your inner critics say and how what they say makes you feel. Don't ask why. That's what trained professionals get paid to help you figure out. Self-diagnosis only gets you so far and rarely alleviates the pain completely.

You will need to convey this info to any professionals you choose to hire so they can accurately diagnose or guide you to a new state of wellness. I encourage you to also consider what you really want, not what the problem is; from where you are to where you want to be. And then find a professional to assist and support you with creating a plan to resolve your issues/problems.

In this moment though, consider it a major win simply to become aware of the voices in your head and trust that there are ways to change the incessant noisy conversations in your mind.

Room to Write, Reflect & Respond

Consider these questions/prompts when and where they're appropriate:

What does this prompt stir in you?

Positive	Negative

What resistance, if any do you feel and where?

For example: Before I speak or make cold-calls I feel a knot in my throat and tightness in my belly.

Old Story	New Story

What if... Consider the worst-case scenario and ask yourself if it's likely to happen or just fear. Then reframe each problem/challenge into an opportunity.

Evaluate the Risks & Rewards of Action/Inaction

Risk	Reward

Action	Inaction

If what you want is necessary and important, decide to act right now.

If not, let it go. Unless or until it becomes important, it's not and is an energy drain.

Ask and Commit

What **one thing** can you do to change/let go of/advance that will make you happier and bring you peace and joy?

Thoughts:

Feelings:

Potential Actions:

Finally, write a Positive Affirmation/Mantra that will help support and manifest your ideal new story.

Enough!
Becoming Brave Enough to Tell Your Inner Critics Off

Whether we admit it or not, we all have a relationship with the critical voices in our heads. Some of these are more dysfunctional than others. Especially when we allow the voices to dictate what we believe about our self-worth and identity; what we are or are not capable of being, doing, or having.

What do some of your inner critics say about you? Is what they are telling you true? Or are they more noise: self-defeating, limiting excuses you continue to believe about yourself and abilities?

Do you believe them? Why? Why not? What would it take to muster the courage to stand up for yourself and tell them off? How would that feel? Do you think you would be happier if you got out of the dysfunctional relationship with them? Why are you still in it? What's stopping you? Or is there a part of you that likes to be belittled? Scoffed at? Unsupported? Told you are *not enough*? A part of you that actually believes their lies—that you will never accomplish your goals or change your bad habits or replace them with better ones?

Into Action/Practice/Get Busy With It:
Take a minute to write down the most frequent criticisms or excuses you hear or believe.

Next comes your defining moment—**do you have the guts to fight back?**

It's time to stand tall look them square into their beady, greedy eyes and boldly declare, **ENOUGH! You don't own me anymore!** Whatever it takes to get you out of your *I can't* hamster wheel mind and onto the superhighway of possibility and inner peace.

Now to make this real, tangible, and actionable, not more puffery with no action, **write your critics a break-up note.**

Look at your list of criticisms and excuses. Imagine them as people you don't like. Why do you still hang out with them? How can you break free from this dysfunctional relationship? Start thinking and journaling about what you want to say to them. Feel all your feelings. Own them.

Then make the decision to end this unhealthy relationship and take a bold step forward. Try it now. If you are angry or sad, you may want to add a few expletives as you write.

Do it now. Write that note. It may be something like this:

I am more than the excuses I make and limitations I have believed about myself. **I am enough.** *As I look over my list of excuses and how I feel when I keep making them, I realize it's time to end this unhealthy toxic relationship that's lasted way too long.*

Goodbye excuses, I don't need you anymore!

Room to Write, Reflect & Respond

Consider these questions/prompts when and where they're appropriate:

What does this prompt stir in you?

Positive	Negative

What resistance, if any do you feel and where?

For example: Before I speak or make cold-calls I feel a knot in my throat and tightness in my belly.

Old Story	New Story

What if... Consider the worst-case scenario and ask yourself if it's likely to happen or just fear. Then reframe each problem/challenge into an opportunity.

Evaluate the Risks & Rewards of Action/Inaction

Risk	Reward

Action	Inaction

If what you want is necessary and important, decide to act right now.

If not, let it go. Unless or until it becomes important, it's not and is an energy drain.

Ask and Commit

What **one thing** can you do to change/let go of/advance that will make you happier and bring you peace and joy?

Thoughts:

Feelings:

Potential Actions:

Finally, write a Positive Affirmation/Mantra that will help support and manifest your ideal new story.

Forgiveness is a Master Key to Finding Inner Peace

Resentments. Anger. Fractured relationships. Being burned. Self-Sabotage. Guilt. Shame. Fear.

All of these are anchors that keep us stuck in unhealthy patterns impeding our ability to find inner peace. Next to developing a consistent gratitude practice and mindset, learning the art of forgiveness is arguably one of the most transformational life and relationship skills we can practice and master.

What does it mean to forgive?

The ninth step of *Alcoholics Anonymous* outlines a very specific way to "make amends" or practice forgiveness as it relates to alcoholics in recovery (If you want, you can buy the book *Alcoholics Anonymous* or you can find a pdf of the pages about the ninth step online). Regardless of your background, I believe the ninth step process can work for anyone who suffers from grudges, anger, deep wounds, and so much more.

Forgiveness is often considered a loaded word because of religious connotations and the inherent pain, guilt, or shame attached to it. Simply put, forgiveness is a process of admitting our shortcomings and misconduct that harmed us or someone else. It is taking personal responsibility to make reparations wherever possible as long as it does not create more pain or suffering.

In my memoir, *Beyond Recovery: A Journey of Grace, Love and Forgiveness* I explore the challenges I faced with learning to forgive my father for leaving me, my two younger brothers, and mom when I was twelve years old. It was a process that took five years of therapy, and multiple attempts over decades to replace my anger and resentment toward my father with love.

Fortunately, I was able to finally heal old wounds before my dad's passing (You'll have to read the book to find out how and why it was so cathartic to me).

My youngest brother, Seth, was not so fortunate. In *Beyond Recovery,* I share a glimpse of his intimate thoughts as he tried to process his own anger and resentment. In his journal dated 9/24/1996, Seth wrote these thoughts: "Who suffers when you refuse to forgive someone?"

"You suffer," he wrote. "Because if you don't forgive you can never be forgiven and also you suffer mentally, physically, and over a period of my life the patterns are a result of not forgiving." Seth also wrote about the emptiness—the hole inside, that many of us have, that needs to be filled with something—drugs, alcohol, food, sex, or ___ fill in the blank.

For many of us, the hole is the need to be recognized, loved or accepted.

In recovery this is referred to as a "God-sized" hole that is best filled by grace, love, faith, and forgiveness—spirituality, or a belief in a "higher power."

What is your "God-sized" hole? What are you doing to fill it? Is that bringing you serenity and peace? If so, great keep doing that. If not, I urge you to continue exploring ways you may learn to not only forgive those who have harmed you but to seek forgiveness to those you have caused harm.

In early recovery, my sponsor told me the first person I needed to forgive was myself.

I continue to practice forgiveness every time I make a mistake or get pissed off at someone or when things don't go my way. Forgiveness is not a one and done solution. It is a way of living that as an alcoholic I must practice daily lest I slip back into my old ways of thinking and acting.

I fully understand that this is not easy for most. But if you are uptight and not nearly as chill as you would like to be, *it may be worth taking a closer look at who you may need to forgive, starting with yourself.*

Room to Write, Reflect & Respond

Consider these questions/prompts when and where they're appropriate:

What does this prompt stir in you?

Positive	Negative

What resistance, if any do you feel and where?

For example: Before I speak or make cold-calls I feel a knot in my throat and tightness in my belly.

Old Story	New Story

What if... Consider the worst-case scenario and ask yourself if it's likely to happen or just fear. Then reframe each problem/challenge into an opportunity.

Evaluate the Risks & Rewards of Action/Inaction

Risk	Reward

Action	Inaction

If what you want is necessary and important, decide to act right now.

If not, let it go. Unless or until it becomes important, it's not and is an energy drain.

Ask and Commit

What **one thing** can you do to change/let go of/advance that will make you happier and bring you peace and joy?

Thoughts:

Feelings:

Potential Actions:

Finally, write a Positive Affirmation/Mantra that will help support and manifest your ideal new story.

Heal Thyself: Love and Be Loved

Love is an act of forgiveness. Grace is the greatest act of love. Empathy and compassion are how we love better.

The problem many face is this: how can we give what we may not feel or believe we have? Must we first learn to love ourselves before we can give love?

Where do we find it, and how do we give it?

You know where the answers are, you only need to live them out loud with arms open wide—put on your own mask first.

What do I mean?

You must learn to love yourself first before you can give love. And yet the paradox is we may need to be willing to be loved by someone else first to teach us this life affirming reciprocal process of giving and receiving.

Nowhere is it more impactful or transformative than though loving and being loved.

If you want to change your life, love more.

Love is the most powerful, healing, and motivational force in the world.

Room to Write, Reflect & Respond

Consider these questions/prompts when and where they're appropriate:

What does this prompt stir in you?

Positive	Negative

What resistance, if any do you feel and where?

For example: Before I speak or make cold-calls I feel a knot in my throat and tightness in my belly.

Old Story	New Story

What if... Consider the worst-case scenario and ask yourself if it's likely to happen or just fear. Then reframe each problem/challenge into an opportunity.

Evaluate the Risks & Rewards of Action/Inaction

Risk	Reward

Action	Inaction

If what you want is necessary and important, decide to act right now.

If not, let it go. Unless or until it becomes important, it's not and is an energy drain.

Ask and Commit

What **one thing** can you do to change/let go of/advance that will make you happier and bring you peace and joy?

Thoughts:

Feelings:

Potential Actions:

Finally, write a Positive Affirmation/Mantra that will help support and manifest your ideal new story.

Plan Your Work and Work Your Plan

Do you wake up in the morning with a plan for your day? Do you write it out the night before? Or do you wake up and start worrying about all the things you have to do that you might forget because you didn't write them down or put them on a calendar?

What do you think about and how do you feel about the day ahead? Do you greet it with gratitude and enthusiasm? Or dread? Which of these mindsets are most common?

Which do you want more of? Perpetual strife and struggle? Or more inner peace, control of your time, or a feeling and sense of accomplishment?

Great, what can you do to create more of what you want and less of what you don't?

Stoke your daily motivation fire with good wood not that green, wet, bay wood that hisses and bubbles because it's not ready to burn, as the bay trees I cut down in my teens to heat our uninsulated home in the winter. Cut and split your wood in the summer and let it season. Prepare for the inevitable storms ahead. As you do, you will sleep better and wake up with a greater sense of comfort, control, and find your days go a whole lot smoother.

These are just a few of many benefits of creating a plan and working that plan.

What's your plan? When will you *start implementing* it or taking the *next step forward to complete it*?

Now is always a good time to start, especially the smallest thing.

Try it and let me know what happens as you start stringing together a series of connected steps. As you do things will likely begin to seem easy, far easier than beating ourselves up about all that we haven't done or "should" do.

Just start here, now. Write down a few things and see how that feels.

Think of this prompt as a test-drive for your dreams and goals.

Go easy on yourself and *start small*.

Room to Write, Reflect & Respond

Consider these questions/prompts when and where they're appropriate:

What does this prompt stir in you?

Positive	Negative

What resistance, if any do you feel and where?

For example: Before I speak or make cold-calls I feel a knot in my throat and tightness in my belly.

Old Story	New Story

What if... Consider the worst-case scenario and ask yourself if it's likely to happen or just fear. Then reframe each problem/challenge into an opportunity.

Evaluate the Risks & Rewards of Action/Inaction

Risk	Reward

Action	Inaction

If what you want is necessary and important, decide to act right now.

If not, let it go. Unless or until it becomes important, it's not and is an energy drain.

Ask and Commit

What **one thing** can you do to change/let go of/advance that will make you happier and bring you peace and joy?

Thoughts:

Feelings:

Potential Actions:

Finally, write a Positive Affirmation/Mantra that will help support and manifest your ideal new story.

Your Attitude Changes Everything

Developing an attitude of gratitude is one of the most liberating, transformational habits we can and should develop, if we want to be happier and enjoy life to the max. On the flip side, as mentioned several times before, feeding our fears, doubts, and worries and perpetuating attitudes or habits of being a victim of circumstance or blaming others for all that we are not, is soul sucking.

I know this may sound harsh, especially when we are in a funk and cannot see a way out of our negative mindset. For some, the hole we seem to have dug for ourselves may seem impossible to escape and may warrant exploring professional guidance in order to break free of our insidious debilitating attitudes. And still, others have become content with being discontent. Resigning themselves to a life of existence, of *it is what it is*. If that brings them joy, so be it. But for me, I want more. I want to feel alive and energized pushing my limits, learning new things. I have been in all of these states at various times in my life. And like the seasonal changes, will likely return to each again and again.

The difference today, after cycling through so many of these seasonal peaks and valleys, of the depressing dark winters and the emergence of new life each spring, is that I know they are coming. To prepare, I stack dry wood for the winter and till the soil in early spring. With each new season I become a little more prepared for whatever may come.

For me, preparation and experience have led to confidence that I can weather virtually any storm. With the exception of the dark and dreary days of winter, which I still let bring me down, I welcome with renewed enthusiasm the shift of each other season.

Each new season offers its own beauty, opportunity, and experiences. My favorite seasons in order are Spring, Summer, and Fall.

Which are your favorites? Least favorite? Which would you like to have a better attitude about? What do you do when you feel down to pick yourself up? Does it help? Do you feel better when you have a good attitude or does a good attitude help you feel better? However, you respond, **if you want to feel better about yourself and life, try a little more gratitude and help someone else. You're gonna like the way you feel, I guarantee it.**

Room to Write, Reflect & Respond

Consider these questions/prompts when and where they're appropriate:

What does this prompt stir in you?

Positive	Negative

What resistance, if any do you feel and where?

For example: Before I speak or make cold-calls I feel a knot in my throat and tightness in my belly.

Old Story	New Story

What if... Consider the worst-case scenario and ask yourself if it's likely to happen or just fear. Then reframe each problem/challenge into an opportunity.

Evaluate the Risks & Rewards of Action/Inaction

Risk	Reward

Action	Inaction

If what you want is necessary and important, decide to act right now.

If not, let it go. Unless or until it becomes important, it's not and is an energy drain.

Ask and Commit

What **one thing** can you do to change/let go of/advance that will make you happier and bring you peace and joy?

Thoughts:

Feelings:

Potential Actions:

Finally, write a Positive Affirmation/Mantra that will help support and manifest your ideal new story.

What's Your One Thing for Today?

If you're anything like me, you likely have a long list of "to do's" running on a continuous loop in your brain. Some are important. Most are loaded with negative emotions, especially if they are things we've been avoiding, procrastinating, making excuses about. Those things are like cancer for our self-image, they tend to bind to each other creating a smokescreen of fear and worry that grows thicker the more we think about them.

Want to clear the mental fog? Pick one thing to do and **get it done, now.**

It can be one of those nagging projects like clearing out your garage or writing your will or doing your taxes. Or it may be something fun that you've been putting off because you have convinced yourself that you are too busy, or don't have the time or money or someone you'd like to share the fun with. Make a decision and go for it.

Into Action/Practice/Get Busy With It:
Find one thing and make a bold decision and act now. Also, remain keenly aware of how doing it makes you feel. What made it so special? How does it feel to actually do what you've been thinking about for so long? Are you lighter? A little happier?

When you return or complete that one thing, whatever it is, write down another. And another. Keep repeating this cycle until it becomes something you want or need to do daily. Something that breathes life and energy into your life.

Once you have developed this discipline, your entire attitude will likely shift. Soon you may bounce out of bed like a kid on Christmas morning who races downstairs to see all the colorfully wrapped gifts placed carefully beneath the tree. For you, every day may be as exciting as it is for a kid at Christmas.

As you continue to cultivate an attitude of gratitude and feeling of accomplishment for doing that one thing daily, your life will never be the same.

Room to Write, Reflect & Respond

Consider these questions/prompts when and where they're appropriate:

What does this prompt stir in you?

Positive	Negative

What resistance, if any do you feel and where?

For example: Before I speak or make cold-calls I feel a knot in my throat and tightness in my belly.

Old Story	New Story

What if… Consider the worst-case scenario and ask yourself if it's likely to happen or just fear. Then reframe each problem/challenge into an opportunity.

Evaluate the Risks & Rewards of Action/Inaction

Risk	Reward

Action	Inaction

If what you want is necessary and important, decide to act right now.

If not, let it go. Unless or until it becomes important, it's not and is an energy drain.

Ask and Commit

What **one thing** can you do to change/let go of/advance that will make you happier and bring you peace and joy?

Thoughts:

Feelings:

Potential Actions:

Finally, write a Positive Affirmation/Mantra that will help support and manifest your ideal new story.

Don't Overthink It

I have so many things in my mind at once I often don't know where to start…

What if I fail? What if it's wrong? What if there's something better? Am I enough? Could I have done better? I should have done or could have done…

STOP! So, what. There will always be someone better than you *and* you can always improve. If you don't think you can improve, then you are just cocky and probably won't be king of the hill for long.

If you fail, that doesn't mean that you are a failure and must wither and cower in a corner like a puppy that peed on the carpet. Just because you came up a little short or didn't win every race, game, contest, award, or whatever, just means you didn't win this time. So what? You're not gonna die.

Short of being obsessive about your work habits and training regimen to get that, be that, do that whatever *that* is, ask *did I do my best?* If not, vow to do better next time. If you are honest and you did give it your all, accept the fact that sometimes your best is not enough to win. Deal with it. Accept it. And ask yourself how bad you want it and whether you are willing to work harder in the future.

Don't overlook the bigger question—*why*. Why do you want it? And what will it mean to you?

Again, when you know your true why, you will not be susceptible to overthinking. You won't be plagued by analysis paralysis of trying to figure out all that went wrong.

When you are determined to succeed, you fall down, bounce back up, change a few things and try again. Better yet, to save yourself some time, find someone who's been where you are and ask for some coaching or guidance to shorten your learning and experience curve.

That's what winners do.

They do not dwell on problems of overthinking everything. *They assess the situation, make adjustments, and get their ass back to work.*

Winners never give up.

They may change direction, but a winner with a white-hot why and a dream will always find a way to make it come true.

Room to Write, Reflect & Respond
Consider these questions/prompts when and where they're appropriate:

What does this prompt stir in you?

Positive	Negative

What resistance, if any do you feel and where?
For example: Before I speak or make cold-calls I feel a knot in my throat and tightness in my belly.

Old Story	New Story

What if... Consider the worst-case scenario and ask yourself if it's likely to happen or just fear. Then reframe each problem/challenge into an opportunity.

Evaluate the Risks & Rewards of Action/Inaction

Risk	Reward

Action	Inaction

If what you want is necessary and important, decide to act right now.

If not, let it go. Unless or until it becomes important, it's not and is an energy drain.

Ask and Commit

What **one thing** can you do to change/let go of/advance that will make you happier and bring you peace and joy?

Thoughts:

Feelings:

Potential Actions:

Finally, write a Positive Affirmation/Mantra that will help support and manifest your ideal new story.

Your Aptitude and Worth are Not Fixed

Let's face it, most of us measure our worth by what we do for a vocation, what we own in terms of cars, toys, how much money we have, the size of our home, our zip code, and what we produce or accomplish. None of these are wrong. But problems arise when we attach our value as human beings to all of these external things.

Doing so can be dangerous especially for those of us who feel we must be perfect to feel good or who give up if we cannot be the best. Far too many of us give in to false beliefs about our lack of skill, ability, and worth, often before even getting started.

Your skills are not fixed. New skills can be learned.

But I have to ask, how painful is it to stay where you are? Are you humble enough to ask for help? Brave enough to change?

What is in the way of you moving past your fear, doubt, worry, and feelings of inadequacy? How can you stop feeling like an imposter? What will make you mad enough to want to change? What do you need to move forward? Are you willing to take a chance on yourself? Or better yet, what if you literally replaced your broken belief system with a newer top-of-the-line model? What would that look like? What would it feel like?

What if you knew you would never ever feel like a failure again because you knew even if it didn't work out as expected the first time, you were one step closer to success?

For those of us who continue to argue for our own limitations, especially when facing unknown challenges with uncertain outcomes, what if we made a simple but profound change in our approach? What if, instead of immediately thinking of all the ways something cannot work, we looked at challenges as a puzzle to be solved? Or instead of comparing our station in life to those we consider to be more successful, smarter, better looking, more talented, etc.—ad nauseum—*what if we asked those who have what we want how they got there?* What did they do? How did they overcome their challenges? Did they have similar setbacks, doubts, fears?

Each and every one of us, unless we have severe mental, physical, or emotional impediments, has the capacity to improve.

Our problems are not due to lack of ability. As mentioned above, skills can be learned and taught. **Our problem is our lack of drive, ambition, and belief.** Like skills, these too can be learned and taught. So, whether you lean toward a fixed scarcity mindset or a growth and abundance mindset, we all have the power to change. **We are only stuck to the degree that we believe we are.**

If you are happy where you are, great. Stay where you are. If not, be bolder and change.

This is a good time to spend a few minutes having a "come-to-Jesus" meeting with yourself. Do a little soul searching and introspection and ask yourself what it will take for you to begin to believe in yourself again? Or, perhaps for the first time ever.

I don't know you, but I do know if you find out why you want something, ask for some help, and become willing and brave enough to get it you will not fail as long as you never give up on you. History is replete with underdog stories. Why not you? Why not now? Are you ready?

Great. Then, let's do this!

Room to Write, Reflect & Respond

Consider these questions/prompts when and where they're appropriate:

What does this prompt stir in you?

Positive	Negative

What resistance, if any do you feel and where?

For example: Before I speak or make cold-calls I feel a knot in my throat and tightness in my belly.

Old Story	New Story

What if... Consider the worst-case scenario and ask yourself if it's likely to happen or just fear. Then reframe each problem/challenge into an opportunity.

Evaluate the Risks & Rewards of Action/Inaction

Risk	Reward

Action	Inaction

If what you want is necessary and important, decide to act right now.

If not, let it go. Unless or until it becomes important, it's not and is an energy drain.

Ask and Commit

What **one thing** can you do to change/let go of/advance that will make you happier and bring you peace and joy?

Thoughts:

Feelings:

Potential Actions:

Finally, write a Positive Affirmation/Mantra that will help support and manifest your ideal new story.

Finish What You Started

I have hundreds of notes on my iPhone in a folder named "Ideas-other." They include everything from book titles and marketing ideas to new concepts for inspiring others, to publishing, coaching, and speaking outlines, plus potential new client prospects my day job.

I do not read them daily; I do not worry that they are not done. I do not fret over having to get through all 983 of them and flush out some 35-point plan and execute a strategy to bring any ideas to fruition.

Why?

Because they are just ideas. Capturing them is the point, until they start to repeat. When that happens, I may explore an idea further, see if it has merit, possibility. And then decide what I'm going to do about it.

I encourage everyone to create some system like this. I've done it for years, but it was best-selling author, Jeff Goins, who suggested we use our phones for this. It's one of the best tools and practices I do, often multiple times a day. What, you may, ask does this have to do with "Finishing what you've started"?

The short answer is everything.

Because I am only concerned with capturing ideas or thoughts, I am not attached to nor do I obsess about feeling like I have to start, research or explore any of them right now. I may later, or not.

Sometimes an idea is more than a brain dump of jumbled concepts, thoughts, or possible outcomes. Sometimes I journal about the first thoughts after meditating or reading something inspiring, uplifting, or interesting. When I do, I let the ideas flow and capture them by writing them down, so they grow roots. This allows my subconscious to organize and investigate whether they are worth further effort.

This system is incredibly helpful for me to not get so distracted by hundreds of other "shiny objects" and maintain focus on more important things such as writing, selling ads, spending time with my wife and our kids, etc. These and other important things, goals, or priorities are what I make sure I invest time in. Complete.

Do I still get distracted by shiny objects? Of course. Don't we all? But one of the keys to finishing what we have started is to spend time doing them every day. As we do, just as working out, we develop muscle, discipline, and healthy habits.

Finishing what we start is really a function of desire, drive, discipline, and persistent focused attention.

Side note: social, relational, or emotional growth, are not tasks to be checked off a to-do list. People are way more important than that. Our growth and maturity in these areas is in direct proportion to time invested, and our humble curiosity for perpetual improvement. Give others and yourself the priority deserved.

With virtually everything else, the key to finishing what you started is really simple: **Prioritize.**

Focus and stop overthinking everything. Just say ***"not now"*** to anything not aligned with what you need to do in this moment.

Lastly, and most important, know why the heck you started it in the first place and what will it mean to you or others when you finish it.

Room to Write, Reflect & Respond

Consider these questions/prompts when and where they're appropriate:

What does this prompt stir in you?

Positive	Negative

What resistance, if any do you feel and where?

For example: Before I speak or make cold-calls I feel a knot in my throat and tightness in my belly.

Old Story	New Story

What if... Consider the worst-case scenario and ask yourself if it's likely to happen or just fear. Then reframe each problem/challenge into an opportunity.

Evaluate the Risks & Rewards of Action/Inaction

Risk	Reward

Action	Inaction

If what you want is necessary and important, decide to act right now.

If not, let it go. Unless or until it becomes important, it's not and is an energy drain.

Ask and Commit

What **one thing** can you do to change/let go of/advance that will make you happier and bring you peace and joy?

Thoughts:

Feelings:

Potential Actions:

Finally, write a Positive Affirmation/Mantra that will help support and manifest your ideal new story.

Final Thoughts:

Remember you can be, have, or do *almost* anything if you want it bad enough and are willing to get out of your comfort zone to work for it. Your motivation to press on despite the inevitable and necessary obstacles of progress, must be born of your inner drive—your reasons why. Without a clearly defined why you will remain susceptible to self-doubt and will likely continue to feel frustrated.

However, the motivational magic of having a reason bigger than any fear, doubt, or obstacle is the spark you'll need to reignite your fire within when you feel like giving up. That magic wand is your white-hot why.

Keep searching until you find what you're looking for. Always keep your why top of mind and make a commitment to a simple yet powerful growth mindset mantra, I will… until.

I will _____ (fill in your blanks), until.

As you make daily progress along the path you have chosen for this leg of your journey, remember to celebrate your wins and give yourself permission to recharge so you don't burnout. **As long as you persist and never give up, you cannot fail.**

Keep putting one foot in front of the other, eyes on the horizon, glancing back occasionally to reflect on how far you've come and for possible clues to continuously improve.

Remember also, *as you go, there you are.*

May you find joy on your journey, wherever it my lead.

Room to Write, Reflect & Respond

Consider these questions/prompts when and where they're appropriate:

What does this prompt stir in you?

Positive	Negative

What resistance, if any do you feel and where?

For example: Before I speak or make cold-calls I feel a knot in my throat and tightness in my belly.

Old Story	New Story

What if... Consider the worst-case scenario and ask yourself if it's likely to happen or just fear. Then reframe each problem/challenge into an opportunity.

Evaluate the Risks & Rewards of Action/Inaction

Risk	Reward

Action	Inaction

If what you want is necessary and important, decide to act right now.
If not, let it go. Unless or until it becomes important, it's not and is an energy drain.

Ask and Commit
What **one thing** can you do to change/let go of/advance that will make you happier and bring you peace and joy?

Thoughts:

Feelings:

Potential Actions:

Finally, write a Positive Affirmation/Mantra that will help support and manifest your ideal new story.

Encouraging Reminders to Memorize and Do Until They Become Habits

Here are some reminders as you tiptoe the tightrope between confidence and humility:
- Remember to do the best you can and appreciate what you have—**be grateful.**
- Ask for help/advice especially when you don't think you need it—**be humble.**
- Find courage within from whatever invisible force inspires and motivates you to change what you can—**be courageous.**
- Tame Your Inner Critics: **Don't feed the beasts!**
- Don't judge yourself or others. Stay in your own lane.
- Don't compare others' success to where you are now.
- **Be patient** with yourself and others. Remember, **progress takes time and effort**
- **Be curious and humble, yet focused and bold.**
- Don't become cocky or complacent because it will undo all the work you've done faster than a fire on a windy day.
- **Think Less. Do More.**
- Resolve to **do a little bit every day.** Whatever it is; Something significant to help you grow in courage and belief.
- **Celebrate success**, no matter how small or large.
- Keep your why alive in your heart and mind.
- **Never give up on your dream.**
- **Never stop learning.**
- Never stop improving.
- **Don't quit before the miracle.**
- Live the mantra, **I will…until.**

Gratitude

Thank you to the many people who have inspired, encouraged, and supported me with your instruction, coaching, kind words, friendship, wisdom, and love throughout my life.

I owe a huge debt of gratitude to Alcoholics Anonymous, my higher power, my sponsor, and those in recovery for teaching me a way of loving and living a fulfilling life free from the chains of addiction.

Thank you to my Redwood Writers family, teachers, therapists, and coaches for teaching me new skills and giving me tools to practice.

Thank you to my mom for loving me when I couldn't love myself. My father for his incessant curiosity and early instruction of spiritual principles which have guided much of my adult life. To my stepfather for pushing me to rise up and be bolder and more confident in my own skills and abilities, and his encouragement for me to never stop learning or improving. For my kids, Andrew, Summer, and Lucas, for giving me an opportunity to lead by example. And lastly for my wife, Crissi Langwell, for her brains, beauty, love, and incredible talent as an author, editor, formatter, and designer. Each of you are the foundational bedrock of this glorious life I get to live.

Thank you!

About the Author

Shawn Langwell is a leader, author, speaker, coach, and award-winning salesperson for the Bay Area News Group, and past salesperson and employee of the year for the New York Times Regional Media Group. He has over three decades of sales experience and thirty-eight plus years of continuous sobriety. In recovery, he has shared his personal story to thousands of people in more than twenty countries around the world.

He is the past president of Toast of Petaluma, and the past president of Redwood Writers, a branch of the California Writers Club, the largest writing club in California. He is the author of the memoir *Beyond Recovery: A Journey of Grace, Love, and Forgiveness* and the recent release, *Ten Seconds of Boldness: The Essential Guide to Solving Problems and Building Self-Confidence* and the accompanying workbook of the same name.

Shawn is also the host of the Dare to Be Great. Dare to Be You Podcast.

His personal mission is to add value to people and businesses everywhere. More specifically, to encourage, inspire, and help people become brave and confident enough to believe they can accomplish their dreams and goals.

Shawn lives in Northern California with his wife author Crissi and Maine Coon cat Cleo.

You can find Shawn at shawnlangwell.com.

Email him at shawnlangwellwriter@gmail.com.

Other Books By Shawn Langwell:

Beyond Recovery: An honest inspirational memoir about overcoming the pain of addiction and alcoholism, resentment, anger, fear, and low self-esteem, and what it took to find sobriety that lasts.

Ten Seconds of Boldness: An inspirational, motivational, and practical self-help guide to stop overthinking, improve self-confidence, and accomplish your personal and professional goals.

Ten Seconds of Boldness outlines a simple yet transformational five-step method to move you from where you are to where you want to be in a way that is purposeful, meaningful, and lasting. Through personal experience and insights from influential leaders across the nation, Shawn Langwell will help you uncover the courage you need to overcome common roadblocks to success such as ***imposter syndrome, fear of failure, fear of success, overthinking, procrastination, and much more.***

Ten Seconds of Boldness Workbook: This practical self-improvement workbook is for those who want a little encouragement, inspiration, and guidance to become bolder and more self-confident.

Speaking, Consulting, or Coaching Requests:

If you or your business are blocked, stagnating, or not reaching your full potential and could use a little inspiration, encouragement, and insight to help you resolve your growth and communication problems, please contact Shawn. His simple five-step approach to solving problems offers a more personalized, creative, and effective strategy than you currently may have.

Email: Shawnlangwellwriter@gmail.com
www.shawnlangwell.com

www.ingramcontent.com/pod-product-compliance
Lightning Source LLC
Chambersburg PA
CBHW060419010526
44118CB00017B/2281